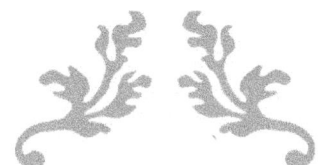

UNLOCKING YOUR PROPHETIC DESTINY

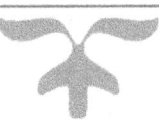

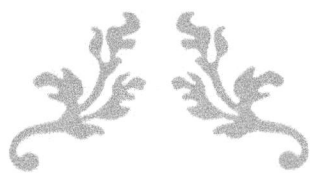

UNLOCKING YOUR PROPHETIC DESTINY

DR. PAMELA SCOTT

UNLOCKING YOUR PROPHETIC DESTINY

Copyright © 2017

Dr. Pamela Scott

Printed in the United States of America

Library of Congress – Catalogued in Publication Data

ISBN: 978-1-949826-80-7

Cover Picture by Linda Harris-Lorio

Cover Design by Eric Culberson

Editorial Assistant: Shavonne Thomas

All rights reserved. No part of this book may be reproduced, stored in a retrieval system, or transmitted in any form or by any means, electronic, mechanical photocopying, recording, or otherwise, without written consent of the publisher except in the case of brief quotations in critical articles or reviews.

Unless otherwise noted, all Scripture quotations are taken from the King James Version Bible.

Endorsements

Dr. Pamela Scott, a prophetess in dance, is pulling the body of Christ into the long- awaited place of movements of the feet of the bride of the Lamb towards the Messiah. This book is a gleaning from heaven's treasury for earth at this hour. She has touched a rare portal that will bring distant questions that have not yet found answers to a closer watch by taking you through the eagle's eye view to the understanding of dance, warfare, priesthood, prophecy and symbols in prophetic dance and art. This is one of the most timely books that the last day church should desire to have in every library and office because there is a dimension and revelation of a victory that can only come when prophetic dance is unlocked in homes and ministries. The King of Kings is coming and the bride will manifest a glorious dance.

Daps Dalyop Gwom
Ancient Floodgate Global Ministry,
Vision Pioneer
Nigeria

Dr. Pamela Scott is an apostolic and prophetic voice to this generation. As a studied professor and an accomplished leader in the field of dance expression, she has impacted many around the world in the areas of fine arts and business. She is the founder and overseer of the Eagles International Training Institute, one of the foremost academies of fine arts training and preparation for ministry to the nations. Also, she is a pastoral leader and a sought-after clinician by many across the globe for her leadership in establishing teams and equipping many to help raise up the next generation of kingdom leaders. In her new book, Dr. Pamela clarifies the role of the prophetic in the life of the believer and its place in creative expression. This book will both challenge and inspire you to grow and to go to higher heights in the Lord! Thank you, Dr. Pamela, for inspiring us to soar again. Eagle nation, Arise!

Pastor Phil Tarver
United Faith Center Ministries International
South Holland, IL.

I am excited to see this new book by Apostle Pamela Scott. It addresses issues that are close to the Lord's heart concerning the progress of His Body on the earth. If the Church does not make a move into the exhortations of this book, it risks missing the fullness the Lord has intended for us this season and instead drifting into beautiful but irrelevant substitutes of His glory. This book brings together the truths God has sewn throughout the Scriptures concerning the arts in ministry and it is a delight to see how Pamela gleans them out and brings them to life.

John Dickson
Worship Leader
Glory of Zion Ministries
Corinth, TX

Table of Contents

Chapter 1
Your Prophetic Destiny.....13

Chapter 2
Living in The Prophetic Dimension...29

Chapter 3
Prophesy from The River...63

Chapter 4
Unlocking the Sounds of God...77

Chapter 5
Worship to Establish His Kingdom...103

Chapter 6
Building Worship Altars...121

Chapter 7
Opening Portals Through Worship...155

Chapter 8
Evangelizing Your Nation Through Worship...177

Chapter 9
Gatekeepers – Prophetic Watchmen...201

Chapter 10
Ecclesia- Arise, Prophesy and Legislate!...221

Chapter 11
Dancing in His Glory...237

1 YOUR PROPHETIC DESTINY

Now is the time for you to unlock the destiny God has planned for you from before the foundations of the earth. It is time for you to dance into your purpose. Timing is knowing when it is God's appointed time. Then, the fulfilling climax of purpose is called destiny.

The kingdom prayer of Jesus is in its last stages of fulfillment. He prayed in Matthew 6:10, "Thy kingdom come. Thy will be done in earth as it is in heaven." He wants His kingdom to first be established in His church, in the hearts of His people. Therefore, we must give Him complete and full reign in our lives.

To see your prophetic destiny fulfilled, you must allow the King to take His domain in every area of your life so His powerful dominion works will be manifested through you. It will require you to become more disciplined under His complete control. He does not want you to continue to live day to day without knowing your prophetic destiny and His progressive purpose for your life.

To see your individual prophetic destiny come to pass, each of us will need to die to self in order, to reveal the life of Christ. We must ask the Lord to show us how to live in present truth, not on the manna of yesterday. Death to self-brings the life of Christ. His process for our lives will be different for each of us and we must submit to His process.

Let's look at the word submission:
- Sub means under
- Mission means assignment

Submission simply means to come under the same assignment or mission. God has a wonderful assignment for you to fulfill in the earth, in order to accomplish the expansion of His kingdom.

You have a personal prophetic destiny. The church has a corporate prophetic destiny and each nation has a prophetic destiny.

Knowing your personal prophetic destiny includes knowing your intrinsic value. Intrinsic value is the actual value of an asset based on both tangible and intangible factors.

In the realm of the Spirit, your intrinsic value has to do with the amazing and unique gifts God has placed inside of you that gives you a divine value unlike anyone else. Once you determine your intrinsic value, you can then begin to live the life He ordained for you.

It's time to unlock your prophetic destiny. To unlock means to undo the lock of (something) by using a key. It also means to make (something previously inaccessible) available for use. We have been given the keys of the kingdom (Matthew 16:19) to unlock the treasures of heaven for ourselves and for others. We have been given access.

This is very exciting, however, unlocking the fullness of your personal prophetic destiny is a process that will move you progressively closer to the abundant life God intends for you. It is not always an overnight manifestation.

Let's look at the life of David. God called him at age 13. Was he the king the next day? No! He was faithfully shepherding his father's sheep.

It was 17 years until he saw even a partial fulfillment of the prophecy that he received when Samuel anointed him and laid hands on him. It was a 24- year process from the time he was anointed to be king by the time he was actually crowned as king.

Yet David remained faithful. David stayed true to God while serving Saul. He was faithful during his times of testing, even when he was on the run because Saul was jealous and wanted to kill him. His destiny was to rule...to be king of all of Israel. Do not give up on the way to your destiny. Maintain your integrity. Remain steadfast. Don't waiver in your faith. Don't lose heart. Do not become weary. Keep a good attitude during your process.

> *God has made promises to you! It is time for you to move into your season of recovery and victory.*

In 1 Samuel 30, David found himself in a place called Ziklag. Ziklag is the place between your promise and your destiny. It is only a temporary season, meant to help you recover your vision. For many, this is a season of recovery.

God made a prophetic promise to David. A prophetic promise from the Lord shifts you into a vision of recovery and victory. God has made promises to you! It is time for you to move into your season of recovery and victory.

Let's take a look at Elisha. Elisha was called to be a prophet but the journey to his destiny called for him to first serve Elijah for 12 years. Who are you serving now? How are you serving now? Where you are serving and how you are serving is directly proportionate to the fulfillment of your destiny.

For 12 years he carried his luggage and prepared his meals. There are no records that Elisha ever performed any miracles or prophesied to anyone on the road to his destiny. Yet he knew that his destiny was tied to the life of Elijah. That's why he told Elijah, "I will not leave you!" So, when Elijah was taken up into heaven Elisha was there to receive the double portion.

Elisha had many opportunities to leave Elijah. If he had left, his 12-year process would not have counted for anything. Yet his faithfulness to the process gained him a double portion and sent him into 50 years of successful ministry.

The process of your prophetic destiny may include tests, trials, setbacks, enemies, misunderstandings, negative circumstances, unjust treatment or rejection.

Things to remember on the road to your destiny:

1. People may not always recognize you but God sees and knows all and will reward you in due season.

2. Do not blame the enemy when a situation or circumstance don't go your way. It could be divinely orchestrated to be part of your destiny. Joseph is a perfect example that righteous acts are not always rewarded immediately but ultimately, his destiny brought him into the palace. He could have gotten

bitter and blamed God for his circumstances. He could have murmured, complained or allowed discouragement to set in. Yet he remained faithful to God and the bible says in Genesis 39:2 that the "LORD was with Joseph..." And God is with you. Even Jesus had a garden process to go through before reaching the throne.

3. Your prophetic destiny is real. It's wonderful. Its God ordained. It's exciting. You may have challenges along the way, but it will be worth it all.

Don't be afraid to go through the birthing canal of adversity. Adversity may be just what is needed to birth you into your new place. Don't mislabel what is happening. The rock and the hard place can look like an attack but it just might be a setup. Ask the Lord to help you understand His ways. Then ask Him to help you walk in obedience.

Do you know what God wants to birth in you? If you are not sure, ask Him! God is upgrading our understanding so we can co-labor with Him. This is a season of continued understanding and revelation.

Gain traction in the Spirit and cultivate your own anointing. Saturate yourself in the oil of His Spirit.

Always follow instructions. Our breakthrough often depends on our ability to follow instructions. Work according to God's blueprint. He does not support other blueprints. Only believe and go forward.

Exodus 14
13 And Moses said unto the people, Fear ye not, stand still, and see the salvation of the LORD, which he will shew to you

today: for the Egyptians whom ye have seen today, ye shall see them again no more forever.

The enemy you have seen you will see no more forever! But there will be new enemies, new tests, new challenges. Don't be mistaken. Don't lose heart. Believe! No more grief! No more discouragement!

Each of us must rise to our destiny. Why is this necessary?

Romans 8
19 For the earnest expectation of the creature waiteth for the manifestation of the sons of God.

The world is waiting for you! Even as Esther was placed in her time to serve her generation, so you have also been born for such a time as this to serve your generation.

Esther 4
14 For if you remain completely silent at this time, relief and deliverance will arise for the Jews from another place, but you and your father's house will perish. Yet who knows whether you have come to the kingdom for such a time as this?"

This is not the time to remain silent. Don't let anyone else dance for you! Don't let anyone else preach for you! Don't let anyone else do what God has called you to do! This is the season for you to arise and shine.

Make up your mind that nothing will stop you from fulfilling your prophetic destiny. Your life, your family, your nation depends on your obedience and your surrender. He has given you His authority to go and change the world!

This is not the time to be afraid!

This is the time to shake off mediocrity!

This is the time to lay down your rights to yourself, even as Esther did!

Don't look for the solution – become the solution your nation needs.

Open your eyes. You will see modern day Josephs and Daniels, Esthers and Davids – rising without compromise and without fear. A greater measure of revelation, faith and overcoming grace is being released to those who will believe!

Corporate Destiny

Now let's look at the corporate destiny. God is a restorer and we are living in a time of God's restoration movement. The ultimate purpose of this restoration is to ultimately see the harvest come in. This prophetic, apostolic movement will release signs, wonders, and miracles in a greater way and each of us has a major part to play in God's end-time plan.

A restoration movement is when God chooses to restore truths to His people. In the past, we saw many restoration movements. Each one paved the way for the next. There has always been a corporate progressive process, from the Protestant movement to the holiness movement, then to the Pentecostal, charismatic and faith movements.

The prophetic movement followed and has paved the way for the apostolic movement. We must understand what God is doing now in His people.

- In the 1950's, the office of the evangelist was restored to the church.
- In the 60's, the role of the pastor was defined and established.
- The 70's brought the restoration of the teacher. Unfortunately, some churches stopped there and failed to see God's progressive purpose.
- But the 80's brought forth the restoration of the prophets. The 90's began to usher in the apostolic reformation which brings a higher level of ministry and anointing.

The corporate destiny of the church is to roar like a lion.

Proverbs 28
1 The wicked flee when no man pursueth: but the righteous are bold as a lion.

To be bold means to trust in God so much and depend on Him so much that you become confident and sure in who He is in you and you know how He chooses to move through you.

Since we are to be as bold as lions, let's look at a few facts about lions.

The male lion and the female lioness each have their own God-given assignment.

Lionesses work well together. Lions protect, lionesses provide. It's the lioness who controls the land, not the lion.

A group of lionesses is called a pride. A coalition of lions leads the pride. It changes every 2-3 years but the lioness remains in her position.

For the lions, their manes frame their face. It represents their authority.

For the lioness, the lack of the mane gives her the ability to blend in with her surroundings almost unseen when stalking her prey. Also, the lack of weight of the mane means she can keep pace and sustain a charge for a longer distance.

Lions know that they need strong, capable lionesses. He does not surround himself with those who are weak and passive hoping to bring them into submission. He looks for a highly specialized, cooperative unit of lionesses.

Lionesses have a keen gift of discernment. They greet and groom each other. They smell each other first because they need to recognize who is or is not part of their group. They have glands on their brows just above their eyes. This is how the scent is released. This is how they identify intruders.

Once another lioness is recognized as part of the pride, they rub their cheeks together and gently butt heads. This shows acceptance and belonging and it strengthens the bonds of affection, seals alliances and exposes impostors.

They greet their cubs by licking their faces. We admonished to greet one another with a holy kiss.

Lionesses groom each other by helping to clean the face and neck and the hard to reach places - they free each other from dirt, ticks, and parasites.

Lionesses are strategic. They work together as a leadership team of strategists. Each has her own role.

When hunting, there are 3 important factors:
　1. Timing
　2. Camouflage
　3. Proximity

They must know when the environment is most favorable for hunting, i.e., at predawn or at dusk?

They are patient and intentional.

Their eyesight remains intact, even at night.

They hide in the open because their color allows them to blend in with open fields. She becomes part of the landscape, thus bluffing her prey into thinking she is nonchalant.

They know she is there but her coolness fools them. At first, the prey is frightened at her presence but once they are comfortable with her presence, she becomes intentional.

She moves in closer as she stays close to the ground. Her paws are soundless. She pauses as she moves closer, then she surprises them by how close she has gotten. Then she pounces on her target.

Lionesses hunt together! As one. Not solo. There is no competition. They do not break rank. They are coordinated at the height of hunting prowess, meaning their ability, skill, expertise, competence, dexterity, aptitude, and proficiency are exceptional.

It has been said that there is nothing more dangerous than being in the presence of lions when they are fully awake.

When lions roar, the atmosphere is changed. Their roars bend back blades of grass and make trees bend to the sound of their roar.

You have a voice! Do not fear the strength of your God! God in you is invincible.

They train their cubs, both male, and female, to hunt. Ezekiel 19:2-3 tells us that they also care for the older and injured lionesses.

Lions rule in the animal kingdom, so we too must rule with the kingdom of God here on the earth.

Numbers 23
24 Behold, the people shall rise up as a great lion.

The word lion has the meaning which implies violence. It is the violent worshippers who rise up like a great lion who will take the kingdom by force.

Matthew 11
12 And from the days of John the Baptist until now the kingdom of heaven suffereth violence, and the violent take it by force.

Your mission

Isaiah 61
1The Spirit of the Lord GOD is upon me; because the LORD hath anointed me to preach good tidings unto the meek; he hath sent me to bind up the brokenhearted, to proclaim liberty to the captives, and the opening of the prison to them that are bound;
2To proclaim the acceptable year of the LORD, and the day of vengeance of our God; to comfort all that mourn;
3To appoint unto them that mourn in Zion, to give unto them beauty for ashes, the oil of joy for mourning, the garment of praise for the spirit of heaviness; that they might be called trees of righteousness, the planting of the LORD, that he might be glorified.
4And they shall build the old wastes, they shall raise up the former desolations, and they shall repair the waste cities, the desolations of many generations.

> *Every generation is looking to be served by the leaders that carry the word for the current move of God.*

The Spirit of the Lord God is upon you and He has anointed you for such a time as this. You have a voice! Determine to go into the destiny God has for you.

- Assess your boundaries. Do they need to change?
- Are you living in the identity God has for you? Do you see yourself as God sees you?
- Are you willing to move out of your comfort zone?
- Are you ready to receive new strategies that will carry you out of old wineskins?
- Will you raise your level of expectation and begin to live each day in the God kind of faith that never waivers?
- Do you know the gifts God has placed in you?
- Do you know the mantle God has placed on your life?

Every generation is looking to be served by the leaders that carry the word for the current move of God. Each of us must align with the revelation in the dispensation of the times in which we live.

You have a voice. People are waiting for you! It is time to fulfill your destiny.

I believe that the fivefold ministry offices mentioned in Ephesians 4 can also be found within the dance ministries, mime ministries and worship ministries in general and for the same purpose – the equipping of the saints.

> *11 And he gave some, apostles; and some, prophets; and some, evangelists; and some, pastors and teachers;*
> *12 For the perfecting of the saints, for the work of the ministry, for the edifying of the body of Christ:*
> *13 Till we all come in the unity of the faith, and of the knowledge of the Son of God, unto a perfect man, unto the measure of the stature of the fulness of Christ:*
> *14 That we henceforth be no more children, tossed to and fro, and carried about with every wind of doctrine, by the sleight of men, and cunning craftiness, whereby they lie in wait to deceive;*
> *15 But speaking the truth in love may grow up into him in all things, which is the head, even Christ:*
> *16 From whom the whole body fitly joined together and compacted by that which every joint supplieth, according to the effectual working in the measure of every part, maketh increase of the body unto the edifying of itself in love.*

The Apostle minister establishes foundations in and out of four walls of a church. Apostles start ministries and raise them up. They cover ministries. They impart fresh revelation and touch all the other ministries. They must live in integrity and holiness. They are called to transform hearts and lives, and to release signs, wonders, and miracles. Apostles gather others and they have the authority to tear down the enemy. They are strong and do not back down. They are pioneers who reproduce spiritual children. They govern, establish and edify the body of Christ.

Prophet ministers have one concern – hearing the voice of God and ministering prophetically according to the heart of God. They dance His messages to the people.

Evangelist ministers use their gifts to reach the lost. Their heart beats for those who do not know Christ and the focus of their mission are to reach out beyond the walls of the church. They also use dance as intercession for the lost.

The pastor minister loves to meet the needs of the dance team with love, they care for them and they know each person in the ministry. They are concerned about the team as well as the needs of the pastor and the congregation.

Teacher ministers use different methods for each audience they are trying to reach. Their heart's desire is to teach the word of God. They love to train, teach, give classes and host workshops and conferences to equip the body of Christ.

Worshippers, know who you are! Rise up and take your place. How? Take hold of His promises for your life.

Proverbs 3
> **5** Trust in the Lord with all thine heart; and lean not unto thine own understanding.
> **6** In all thy ways acknowledge Him, and He shall direct your paths.

Our expectations are often too low. We often look with earthly eyes instead of using our faith to unlock the treasures of heaven! Your mindset will determine your destiny! Change your mindset, change your destiny.

Destiny of A Nation

The destiny of a nation depends on the people of God who live in that nation. It is up to us to be good stewards of the nation in which we live. Many of us are called to be a steward of other nations as well.

In order, to dance the prophetic destiny of your nation, you must first carry God's heart for the nation. Ask God to give you His heart for our nation. I will discuss this further in a later chapter.

Learn to govern in your sphere. Let passion rise up in you and take possession of your destiny. You are strong in the power of His might. That's what God says about you. You were made in His image and you have His DNA. You were created in His likeness. He gave you dominion. Because God lives in you, you can live in victory and dance into your prophetic destiny.

ACTION:

Here are the "ABC's of My Prophetic Destiny." On average, it takes more than **2 months** before a new behavior becomes automatic — 66 days to be exact. And how long it takes a new habit to form can vary widely depending on the behavior, the person, and the circumstances. Research shows that it can take anywhere from 18 days to 254 days to form a new habit.

So, say the ABC's daily out loud until a habit forms in your behavior and in your thought processes.

Acknowledge God. He makes all things unlimited my life. The power of God is in me and I carry His power.

Believe that I am who He says I am. I have the ability, to be fruitful and multiply.

Choose His life. Don't settle for what life brings or for what others say. His power in me assures me that I will live His abundant life every day!

- Determine to rule MY world. If I don't, who will?
- Encourage myself in the Lord daily for spiritual strength.
- Faith in God. I believe that with my God, all things are possible,
- Glorify God! Then He will do the impossible. Possibilities are coming my way.
- Hear from heaven, then I will declare it in the earth.
- In Jesus Christ, I place my trust. He is my way, my truth, and my life.

Judge not the things I do not understand. Ask God and obey.

Keep myself in the love of God by praying in the Holy Ghost according to Jude vs. 20.

Love the Lord my God will all my heart, and with all my soul and with all my mind.

Miracles are mine! I believe!

Now faith is the faith I live by and it is the substance of things hoped for!

Observe to do all that is written in the word of God.

Pray without ceasing!

Quality time spent with God is more valuable than all the jewels in the world.

Rest in the Lord and wait patiently for Him.

See it! If I can see it, I can have it.

Treat others as I would like to be treated!

Unique! I am Unique!

Victory is mine! It has already been won for me!

Winner! I am already a winner.

Expand the kingdom of God daily.
Yes! Jesus loves me!

Zealous! Be zealous for good works!

2 THE PROPHETIC DIMENSION

To access our prophetic destiny, we must learn to live in the prophetic dimension. The prophetic dimension is so important.

Amos 3

7 Surely the Lord GOD will do nothing, but he reveals his secret unto his servants the prophets.

Prophets are so important that God has decreed that he will do nothing or say nothing without them. You may or may not have the office of the prophet but you must be a prophetic believer.

Now is the time for the prophets and God's prophetic people to arise. Arise! Arise!

There is a prophetic generation who must come forth in the last days, those who will call God's people back to holiness and righteousness...those who will say what God is saying, not what they think people want to hear.

The Spirit of Prophecy

Revelation 19

10 And I fell at his feet to worship him. And he said unto me, See, thou do it not: I am thy fellow-servant, and of thy brethren that have the testimony of Jesus: worship God: for the testimony of Jesus is the spirit of prophecy.

To prophesy means:
1. To speak by divine inspiration
2. To foretell that which is to come about a future event
3. To forth-tell, as in telling a truth
4. To agree with what God has already said to be true in his word

There are three areas of prophetic ministry:
1. The office of the prophet...person who has been anointed to be a spokesperson for God....a five-fold ministry gift mentioned in Ephesians 4:11:

And he gave some, apostles; and some, prophets; and some, evangelists; and some, pastors and teachers;

2. According to 1 Corinthians 12, the gift of prophecy: a gift of divine gratuity - a spiritual endowment and empowerment - a spiritual qualification.

   7But the manifestation of the Spirit Is given to every man to profit withal.
   8For to one is given by the Spirit the word of wisdom; to another the word of knowledge by the same Spirit;
   9To another faith by the same Spirit; to another the gifts of healing by the same Spirit;
   10To another the working of miracles; to another prophecy; to another discerning of spirits; to another divers kind of tongues; to another the interpretation of tongues:
   11But all these worketh that one and the selfsame Spirit, dividing to every man severally as he will.

3. The Spirit of prophecy as mentioned in Revelation 19:10. It is the spiritual condition of an atmosphere that is conducive to the speaking forth (dancing, singing, painting, drawing, sculpting or other creative expressions) of God's word, not based on gift or office. Every believer can function at this level of Revelation.

Acts 2 gives us, even more, insight into the prophetic God has placed on the body of Christ.

16 But this is that which was spoken by the prophet Joel;
17 And it shall come to pass in the last days, saith God, I will pour out of my Spirit upon all flesh: and your sons and your daughters shall prophesy, and your young men shall see visions, and your old men shall dream dreams:
18 And on my servants and on my hand maidens I will pour out in those days of my Spirit; and they shall prophesy:

The 3-fold Purpose of Prophecy

1 Corinthians 14
> **1** Follow after charity, and desire spiritual gifts, but rather that ye may prophesy.
> **2** For he that speaketh in an unknown tongue speaketh not unto men, but unto God: for no man understandeth him; howbeit in the spirit he speaketh mysteries.
> **3** But he that prophesieth speaketh unto men to edification, and exhortation, and comfort.
> **4** He that speaketh in an unknown tongue edifieth himself; but he that prophesieth edifieth the church.
> **5** I would that ye all spake with tongues, but rather that ye prophesied: for greater is he that prophesieth than he that speaketh with tongues, except he interprets, that the church may receive edifying.

> To edify means to build up.

> To exhort means to encourage.

> To comfort means to offer consolation.

Verse 1 makes it clear that we should desire to prophesy. We should speak in tongues. Many people are still not filled with the power God wants them to have. When we speak in tongues, according to verse 2, in the spirit, we speak mysteries.

If the enemy cannot move you out of the church, he will deceive you while you are in the church. Many are still dancing, but have no power because they have allowed themselves to live under the structure of an old wineskin.

As I travel, I hear people say the same thing over and over. They say, "I don't believe in speaking in tongues."

"My church doesn't believe in it. My pastor does not believe in it."

"If God wants me to have it, He will give it to me."

" I'm not good enough."

That is old wineskin, religious thinking. If that is your thinking, let God break it off of you. Read and receive the words of Jesus.

John 7

> **37** In the last day, that great day of the feast, Jesus stood and cried, saying, If any man thirst, let him come unto me, and drink.

> **38** He that believeth on me, as the scripture hath said, out of his belly shall flow rivers of living water.
> **39** (But this spake he of the Spirit, which they that believe on him should receive: for the Holy Ghost was not yet given; because that Jesus was not yet glorified.)

There are rivers of living water inside of you! Let the rivers flow!

The River of God brings change. That's why the enemy lies to you about it.

Acts 1
> **8** But ye shall receive power, after that the Holy Ghost is come upon you: and ye shall be witnesses unto me both in Jerusalem, and in all Judaea, and in Samaria, and unto the uttermost part of the earth.

Power is the word Dunamis, where we get the word dynamite. It means force, miraculous power, abundance, strong and mighty worker of miracles.

He also gives us Exousia.

Luke 10
> **19** Behold, I give unto you power (Exousia) to tread on serpents and scorpions, and over all the power (Dunamis) of the enemy: and nothing shall by any means hurt you.

This word means privilege, capacity, competency, freedom, superhuman, delegated influence, authority, jurisdiction and right.

You must know who you are!

You have Dunamis and Exousia.

On the Day of Pentecost, the outpouring of the Holy Spirit came.

When the outpouring of the Spirit came, the 120 followers of Jesus who were gathered together in the upper room were all filled with the Spirit and began to praise God in other tongues.
People thought they were drunk. Peter stood up and boldly set the record straight. The disciples were not drunk at all, but this was a fulfillment of Joel's great prophecy.

Acts 2
> **16** But this is that which was spoken by the prophet Joel;
> **17** And it shall come to pass in the last days, saith God, I will pour out of my Spirit upon all flesh: and your sons and your daughters shall prophesy, and your young men shall see visions, and your old men shall dream dreams:
> **18** And on my servants and on my hand maidens I will pour out in those days of my Spirit, and they shall prophesy.

The disciples went forth and turned the world upside down with that power!

Jude
> **20** But ye, beloved, building up yourselves on your most holy faith, praying in the Holy Ghost,

21 Keep yourselves in the love of God, looking for the mercy of our Lord Jesus Christ unto eternal life.

You need to edify yourself daily!!! You need to live and walk in God's power...how often? Everyday!

So, receive the power of God in a new way so you can be free to release the prophetic.

How do we live in the prophetic dimension?

1. Preaching the word of God. You can prophesy with words.

2. Singing the words and sounds of God. You can prophesy in song and in sound.

3. Dancers move to demonstrate prophetic words and sounds. You can prophesy in movement. Dance is Holy Spirit speaking.

4. Prophetic art can be release through painting, sculpting and other various creative expressions.

5. The prophetic can be released through flags, banners, streamers, mime and other creative art forms.

God's house, (that's us) both spiritual and natural, should be the place known in every city, state and nation as a place for prophetic ministry, healing and transformational impact.

If we are to see a culture of prophetic revelation flourish in the body of Christ, we must align our vision of God's house with His vision of His house.

God's house is not self-centered. God's house is designed to be a source of life, blessing, and change for all the nations of the earth.

Many people in the church are much too focused on themselves. Many go to the altar for the same thing week after week. That should not be so.

Freedom has been won for us! Only free people can FREE people.

It's not all about me, me, me or you, you, you. It is about Jesus and what He wants to say and do in the earth. Through prophecy, we bring heaven to earth. Prophecy is for men so we hear from heaven, and release it in the earth.

His kingdom comes as we prophesy according to His word, His will, and His purpose. He will watch over His word to perform it.

You need to be in a body of believers that not only understands the prophetic but allows true prophetic release.

Why is this important?

1. God is always speaking. The question is, are we listening to what He wants to say or do we move forward with our own agendas, edging God out (ego) with announcements and man-made programs that have no life?

The true prophetic anointing will not allow you to stay in an old wineskin that lacks the power needed for victory.
You need a now word. Not just a testimony of what God said to you 5 years ago. God has fresh revelation for us.

The children of Israel had to follow the cloud of God's presence daily for protection and for provision.

God has sounds He has not even released into the earth. Prophetic churches understand how to hear and steward the sounds of God.

Deliverance, joy, and hope are sounds that bring freedom to entire nations.

You cannot live new life with old sounds or old songs. New songs break old cycles.

Prophetic churches know how to work with a prophetic, apostolic anointing in order to train you so they can send you to do the work of the kingdom.

You were not born to warm a pew. True prophetic churches will not allow you to sit and warm a pew.

Cutting edge prophetic churches understand that they have a mandate from heaven to change not only families but cities, states, and nations.

Cutting edge prophetic churches will expand your vision to include all people, every tribe, and every tongue.

2. Pure prophecy purifies the church and challenges you in the spirit of Elijah. Elijah asked Israel the same question we need to ask today, "How long will you halt between two opinions? If the Lord is God, serve Him."

The Bible says the people "answered him not a word."

The word halt means to do a limping dance. You cannot limp between the church and the world. You cannot contaminate yourself in the world and come to dance in the presence of a Holy God.

> *The word halt means to do a limping dance. You cannot limp between the church and the world.*

Your entire life matters. Your attitude matters. Your motives matter. How you respond when you are challenged or faced with things that may not go your way matters. Every Facebook post matters. What you allow in your eye and ear gates matters.

Where is your fruit? Are you working to cultivate the fruit of the Spirit? "Love, joy, peace, long-suffering, gentleness, goodness, meekness and temperance..." Galatians 5:22.

How can you hear God if you allow sin to enter your temple so easily?

3. True prophecy can bring proper judgment that results in the church being a living epistle. True prophecy also prepares the bride to be the glorious church of Jesus Christ!

Titus 2

12 Teaching us that, denying ungodliness and worldly lusts, we should live soberly, righteously, and godly, in this present world;

Colossians 3

5 Mortify (put to death) your members which are upon the earth; fornication, uncleanness, inordinate affection, evil concupiscence, and covetousness, which is idolatry:
6 For which things' sake the wrath of God cometh on the children of disobedience:
7 In the which ye also walked some time, when ye lived in them.
8 But now ye also put off all these; anger, wrath, malice, blasphemy, filthy communication out of your mouth.
9 Lie not one to another, seeing that ye have put off the old man with his deeds;
10 And have put on the new man, which is renewed in knowledge after the image of him that created him:
13 Forbear one another and forgive one another...if any man have a quarrel against any: even as Christ forgave you, so also do ye.

How can we say that we cannot forgive someone when God has forgiven us of our many sins?

Someone asked my husband, "Is it possible to forgive someone but never speak to them again?" His reply was, "What if Jesus did that to you?"

Let's grow up sons of God!

Colossians 3
> **14** And above all these things put on LOVE charity, which is the bond of perfectness.
> **15** And let the peace of God rule in your hearts, to the which also ye are called in one body; AND 'be ye thankful.
> 16. And let the word of Christ dwell in you richly.

What do we need to know about flowing in prophetic expression?

- Know the word of God. When we know the word of God, we can obey the word of God.

- Know that 1 Chronicles 15 tells us that we have been appointed as carriers of the ark of his presence. Be a carrier of the ark.

- 1 Thessalonians 5:20 tells not to despise prophecies.

- Romans 12
  > **6** Having then gifts differing according to the grace that is given to us, whether prophecy, let us prophesy according to the proportion of faith;

Check the motives of the heart. Salome danced before King Herod and pleased the King so much that she was able to ask for and to receive the head of John the Baptist. Let's make sure the motives of our heart please the King of Kings.

-Learn to listen to Holy Spirit.

John 10
27 My sheep hear my voice, and I know them, and they follow me:

-Know when to dance. Move out as the Lord leads and guides. -According to my dear friend Vivien Hibbert:
-Dancers are carriers of the sights of God
-Musicians are carriers of the sounds of God
-Psalmists are carriers of the words of God

Submission to leadership is a must, both dance leaders as well as church leaders. If you have authority issues, be honest with yourself and deal with it. Otherwise, you leave yourself open to lies and attacks from the enemy. The anointing is on the head and it flows down. It can be spiritually dangerous if you are out of alignment because you think you know more than your leader or you don't agree with what you have been instructed to do or you allow offense to move you out of place. It could have an impact on your destiny.

Prophecy can come to you:

- As an impression or feeling
- Before, during or after a prophetic word
- As a small, still voice
- As an internal audible voice
- As an audible voice
- As a response to a sermon or teaching
- In a vision

The purposes of prophetic expression in the church include:

1. To establish God's kingdom - Joshua 1:3, Psalms 18:40, Malachi 4:3, Luke 10:19
2. To express joy and victory - Exodus 15:20
3. To express victory through shouting - Psalm 47:1
4. To lead others into praise and victory - Exodus 15:20
5. To rejoice and usher in God's presence - 2 Samuel 6:14-16, 1Chronicles 15:29
6. As worshippers gathered together - Psalms 149:3, 150:4
7. To release healing and deliverance - Isaiah 58:6... (Nathan, to shake, to let loose, to untie)
8. To lead into battle - 2 Chronicles 20
9. To triumph over the enemy - Colossians 2:15 - a declamatory march or procession
10. To show worship and humility - Psalm 95:6 (Barak, to bow down)
11. To clap hands over the enemy - Psalm 47:1

Prophetic ministry takes place in three realms:

1. In Heaven to God – we let Him know that we agree with His prophetic word over our lives. For example, Psalm 23:1 could read as follows – Lord, I agree that you are my shepherd, I shall not want.
2. Unto principalities and powers. Ephesians 3:**10:** *To the intent that now unto the principalities and powers in heavenly*

> *places might be known by the church the manifold wisdom of God,*

3. In the earth realm...Jeremiah 29:11 could read: Lord, thank you that you have good plans for me, plans to prosper me, not to harm me...plans to give me hope and a future.

According to 1 Samuel 30:6, "David encouraged himself in the Lord." Therefore, you can edify, exhort and encourage yourself and others.

Using instruments to accompany prophetic movements is a must as we learn to become visual demonstrations of what God is saying and of what He wants to display in the earth. Here are some examples of what can be used to give sight to the word of God:

- Sword
- Shield
- Cloth
- Bible
- Mattah
- Tambourine
- Candle
- Billow
- Flag
- Banner
- Rain stick
- Crown
- Scepter
- Streamer

It is also necessary to understand the prophetic meaning of colors. The "tabernacle colors." taken from Exodus 28, are blue, purple, gold and scarlet. So, colors have a prophetic dimension. Here is a brief list of colors and what they represent:

Gold-Deity of Christ, glory
Silver-Redemption
Black-Death, void
Green- Everlasting life, prosperity
Purple-Royalty
Scarlet- Passion of Christ
Blue- Heavenly, refreshing, river, Holy Spirit
White- Holiness, purity, light, righteousness
Red- Blood of Jesus
Orange- Prophetic
Pink- Right relationships
Bronze-Refining

Discerning the Times

We all should be able to discern the times and know where we are on God's timetable. His timetable is not the same as ours. In fact, we are the ones who live in time. God is not bound by time. He does not live in time.

God doesn't want us to be caught unaware of what He is doing.

Every church should have a prophet who hears from God and releases what He says and reveals what He is doing.

There are prophets who are called to hear God for specific churches, others are called to specific regions, and others are called as prophets to nations.

You may not be called to the office of the prophet but you must have ears to hear what God is saying.

From the first moments of human history, God has spoken to and taught his children by prophets and he has never gone away from that pattern.

A prophet is God's mouthpiece and messenger to make known his divine will. Therefore, a prophet's word is meant to be God's word.

Amos 3

8 The lion hath roared, who will not fear? the Lord GOD hath spoken, who can but prophesy?

This has two parts. Let's look at the first part.

Let's look at the lion's roar.

A lion's roar is one of the loudest noises any animal on Earth can make. It is so loud that it can be heard over five miles away.

They roar to establish their presence in a territory. Roaring is a strong form of communication to show ownership of their territory. They also roar when they are mad.

It's time to announce that a lion is in our midst! The Lion of the tribe of Judah!

In order for lions to roar effectively, they must first change their posture. The release of such a strong declaration of might requires a bow. Their heads drop, and they expand their chests in order to fill their lungs with air.

Likewise, if we are ever going to produce a sound of such magnitude, that it will change atmospheres, it will require a change in our present posture. To have the ability to roar, we must drop our pride and bow down. Humble ourselves before God. Humility and prayer will position us to receive a fresh infilling of the breath of God's Spirit.

The power of a lion's roar can surround you and stop you in your tracks.

It's He who roars through us! The world will hear His roar.

Our world is filled with roars. Oceans roar. The wind roars. Waterfalls roar.

But Our God Most High, the Lord of all...He Himself roars.

Jeremiah 25
>**30** GOD roars like a lion from high heaven;
>thunder rolls out from his holy dwelling.

Hosea 11
>**10** The people will end up following GOD.
>I will roar like a lion—Oh, how I'll roar!
>My frightened children will come running from the west.

Joel 3
>**16** The LORD will roar from Zion and thunder from Jerusalem; the earth and the heavens will tremble. But the LORD will be a refuge for his people, a stronghold for the people of Israel.

He roars when we worship! When we praise! When we shout!

Our response to the revelation God is giving in this hour should be a devoted heart set to prophesy His word. Until we speak forth that which God has revealed, how can people hear?

But when we speak, the Holy Spirit can create the reality of His word and His will through us. The lion hath roared, who will not fear?

As when a lion roars, no one who hears can avoid being afraid.

When God speaks, all who hear should stand in awe.

The Lord God hath spoken, who can but prophesy? When God Himself speaks, or commands, who would dare to do anything other than obey?

What prophet would dare to refuse to say what God reveals to him, and commands him to speak?

If the anger of a lion is to be feared, how much more the voice of God? The Lord God hath spoken, who can but prophesy?

It's the Lion of the tribe of Judah that is roaring.

Proverbs 28:1
The righteous are as bold as a lion.

Jeremiah said the Word in his heart was like a fire shut up in his bones (Jer.20:9).

The fire that burned in Jeremiah's heart was powerful. He could not help but prophesy.

The Lord is speaking to the Body of Christ as He spoke to Jeremiah of old. It's a time to root out, to pull down, to destroy and throw down, to build and to plant.

Unless we as the Body of Christ are the channels of His voice, how will the world hear? It's time to be the voice of God in the earth.

What has God spoken and what are we to prophesy?

Here are <u>5 prophetic paradigms</u> that were released at Glory of Zion International (www.gloryofzion.org) that I believe are key for this season:

1. Align with God and Keep in Step!

> We must be aligned with God to properly hear and see. Ask God to awaken your senses to Him.
>
> This is our time to get in step...keep rank... with Lord Sabbaoth, the Lord of an army......it's time to submit to His leading.
>
> God said, "In the midst of the chaos around, you can know the leadings and the touch of My Spirit. Be ready to walk in triumph.
>
> Put one foot in front of you and then from behind you will hear My voice telling you which way to go.

For I am changing directions of many of My people at this time; if you keep going, you would find yourself at a dead end.

But if you will listen carefully then you will walk my way and into the victory that I have planned.

For I have an army coming together, and even though they are disjointed and even though they are scattered, they are hearing and forming the way I have chosen.

Take hands. Watch and pray, for I will set people on your path that give you directions over how to get in rhythm for your future.

You will find it unusual who you will align with, in days ahead and you will find it strange who you call and how you synergize with those that I put in your path.

I will cause Your enemies to even provide for you in days ahead.

So, get ready, for I have a people that are coming together to move throughout the earth!"

ACTION

Dance and SHOUT, "Amen! Let it be Lord!"

2. Embrace the New Wineskin

This year is about embracing what heaven is bringing.

Embrace the year ahead.

It's time to War for His glory and let His glory war for you!

Only His glory will shift the warfare you face.

God is Opening realms of heaven.

He is opening portals to cause the host of heaven to align with armies of heaven.

War violently over kingdom purpose.

He is unlocking an identity in you that has been locked up.

It's time to recover your true identity and transform into the new identity God has for you and not the identity you have put on for yourself.

You must overcome to experience a new glory.

Let His glory invade your portion.

Allow His glory to manifest.

When the glory is unlocked the flesh will not rule.

The flesh is not what God wants to rule your life.

Place hands on spirit man and shout......UNLOCK

Look and see How your will is aligning with His will.

It's time for new wineskin

Luke 5

37 And no man putteth new wine into old bottles; else the new wine will burst the bottles, and be spilled, and the bottles shall perish.

38 But new wine must be put into new bottles, and both are preserved.

39 No man also having drunk old wine straightway desireth new: for he saith, the old is better.

If you keep drinking the old wine you won't desire the new. You will keep thinking that the old is ok.

If you keep living the same way, thinking the same way, acting the same way, dancing the same way, you cannot answer the higher call.

Evaluate your life. When confronted with a situation, if you address it the same way, ask yourself if you are ready to receive the new wine, to become a new wineskin.

Don't resort to your old ways. With the new wineskin, mentality comes authority, revelation, and direction.

Answer the call. Let go of the old. Let go of old attitudes. Let go of old ways. Let the old mentality go! Fear must go! Lack of confidence must go! Selfishness must go!

You can't-do the old and expect the new. Choose to embrace the new. He will pour in new wine.

- ❖ Let go of the old thoughts.

- ❖ Let go of old expectations.

- ❖ Let go of old attitudes.

- ❖ Let go of old ways.

- ❖ Let the old mentality go!

- ❖ Fear must go!

- ❖ Let go of hurt.

- ❖ Lack of confidence must go!

- ❖ Selfishness must go!

- ❖ You can't-do the old and expect the new.

Choose to embrace the new. He will pour in new wine.

John the Baptist preached a necessary and relevant message as a forerunner to Jesus.

When the time came for Jesus to begin His ministry, John had to decrease so the ministry of Jesus could increase.

It was time for a new wineskin. The followers of John had to shift.

They had no choice. We have no choice but to shift.

Many churches are still operating under an old wineskin.

The transition from an old system to new system is not always easy but it is necessary if we are to stay in the timing of God.

- Shift from an old method to new method!
- Shift from an old paradigm to new!
- Shift from religion to kingdom!

Welcome His new dimensions in every area your life!

- Welcome new sight.
- Welcome new strength.

- Welcome the new wineskin.

Are you allowing the new wineskin to manifest in and through you?

The new wineskin will change your life and the lives of those you touch.

As you receive the new wine, you can pour out new wine.

ACTION

Dance releases you of the old things. Then SHOUT, "I am shifting into the new things God has for me!"

3. No More Delay

Many of God's people will also have a new and sudden awakening of their spiritual gifts, talents, and purpose that will produce the manifestation of sudden miracles, signs, and wonders.

Things that were out of place will snap back into place.

The stage that is set is for the "new spiritual awakening" and revival for lost souls to enter the kingdom of God!

We are living in the time of supernatural acceleration. Things that used to take 10 years, can now manifest in 10 months, 10 days, 10 hours, 10 minutes or even 10 seconds.

Seeds that were sown in past are now ready for reaping.

No more hope deferred! No more delay! It is possible to start living in the supernatural realm.

God is supernatural, we have His DNA so we are also supernatural.

That's what prophetic is. That's what worship is. Eternal....outside of the constraints of time...

Luke 4
18 The spirit of the lord is upon me, for he has anointed me to bring good news to the poor. He has sent me to proclaim that captives will be released, that the blind will see, that the oppressed will be set free...."

The Lord said:

"I am raising up prophetic voices to declare My glory to this generation. They will be those who will trumpet My words with clarity and precision as they minister in the Spirit and power of Elijah.

They will turn the hearts of the fathers to the children, and the disobedient to the wisdom of the just. They will prepare the people's hearts for the days ahead.

They will be men and women who will walk in the anointing as in days of old. There will be miracles, signs, and wonders performed through their hands as My anointing rests upon them and abides within them.

They will show others how to be fed supernaturally in the times of famine. They shall decree a thing and it shall be established because I will confirm the words that I give them to speak.

They are men and women of valor who follow in the steps of My prophets who went before them.

They are those who have put their hand to the plow and have not looked back.

They are those who have never deviated from My plan but have followed Me through difficult times and persecution.

They will bring reconciliation to My body and bring every joint and ligament to function in unity.

I am raising up men and women who know how to take back their land.

They will take a stand against unrighteousness, sin, and injustice, and they will be steadfast in their convictions,

There will be unbelievers in the days ahead who will not understand the call on the lives of My prophets. They will be mocked and ridiculed as My servants but they will not retreat.

Those who I have called, I will also equip with strength and endurance. I will give them divine wisdom with spiritual strategies.

They will understand the times and the seasons, and walk accordingly. I will give them keen discernment concerning their ministry and the sword of My word will be in their mouths.

They will bring truth to the body and bring unity in places of division.

They will walk in righteousness but not submit to the religious traditions of man because they are led by My Spirit. Supernatural encounters and signs will follow those who believe as I am raising up mighty men and women in the spirit of Elijah, says the Lord."

If you read that and you He is talking about you, receive it!

ACTION

Dance, sing and SHOUT, "Lord, let it be me!"

A word for those in the marketplace:

"This is the time where transition will occur in the marketplace from mending nets to making networks. There will be a convergence of a new breed of people who will enter the financial arena working with groups who walk in demonstration carrying a depth of revelation concerning multiplication and increase. In the midst of this strong fusion will come a new flow of Holy Ghost power in the marketplace.

This year brings with it a reality that will break the yoke of delusion off the minds of God's people. Many will awake from the reality of what they feared they could not overcome to find that the delusion has been cleared like a smoke and the way out revealed.

The chains will be broken and many will feel as if they awoke from a deep sleep. For I am removing the sting of past experiences to help you fulfill accomplishments that you could not do on your own.

Mark this time, because you will witness this year how I will transform time, move through time, and even redeem time in your lives."

Position yourself. God will release keys so that we will forge ahead no matter what is opposing us. Timing will play a key factor in how your destiny plays out. Be sensitive to His leading and be quick to obey. Do not delay. Many things will happen in accelerated moments of time.

4. Position Yourself and Stand

You will need His instructions as you will find yourselves transitioning into the supernatural place God has called for us to be.

So much ground has been covered and what we perceived to be lost has truly been a time of gaining.

The Lord will begin to release biblical downloads and supernatural blueprints with your answers.

Stop and ask right now for His biblical downloads and supernatural blueprints!

These prophetic signs will help you proceed on our journey forward toward your destiny.
You have not been waiting in vain, nor are you standing still while in pursuit of all that God is preparing for you.

Now is the time to stand - stand in the knowing. The knowing is a place where the opinions of others and even ourselves has no power to affect our stand on the truth of the promises of God.

It's time for us to know what God is saying and to remember the manner in which God is saying it.

Observe with discerning eyes what is going on around us. Proceed from the place of knowing that your very life is hidden with Christ in God.

ACTION

Dance unto the Lord and ask for His strategies for your life.

5. Paradigm Shifts

Lastly, we must prophesy paradigm shifts. Repeat each of these out loud.

-Lord, show me which of my current paradigms must change. Then give me the wisdom to make the changes. Change does not mean the old was wrong. It's just time for different strategies for new season. My strategies must change radically. This will produce the fruit I have been expecting!

-I will no longer live in my comfort zones.

-Father, expose where I have submitted to the spirit of religion. I will let go of my old wineskins. I submit to your plan for your destiny.

-I receive a new measure of faith to move in supernatural. I receive an increase in signs, wonders, and miracles in my life. My kingdom boundaries will increase.

ACTION

Dance out of your comfort zone into a new place of faith!

NOTE: If you need to receive emotional healing, including the need to forgive and release things that you could not understand, do it now so it will not weaken you in days ahead. There is a wonderful book titled Set Yourself Free by Dr. Robert Heidler. You can find it at www.gloryofzion.org. It is your time to live in freedom!

3 PROPHETIC FROM THE RIVER

Revelation 22

1 And he shewed me a pure river of water of life, clear as crystal, proceeding out of the throne of God and of the Lamb.
2 In the midst of the street of it, and on either side of the river, was there the tree of life, which bare twelve manners of fruits, and yielded her fruit every month: and the leaves of the tree were for the healing of the nations.

This river is pure and clean. Nothing contaminated and nothing unclean is in this river.

The waters of life are alive and it causes you to live! This river flows from throne of God, from His supreme deity.

In order to flow in this river, you must remain properly positioned at the throne of God.

If you do not remain at the throne of God, you can find yourself in any river. Other rivers could take you off of the course He has for you. Rivers of:

- Religion
- Lack
- Confusion
- Depression
- Discontent
- No revelation

There is a river of life that releases blessings and breakthrough. This is the river needed to take you to destiny.

This river flows from throne, not from the cross.

Both the cross and the throne are needed. We need the power of finished work of the cross as well as the grace of the throne.

We have access to throne! Why stay in wilderness when the throne is available?

Hebrews
>**16** come boldly unto the throne of grace....

Ephesians 2
>**6** And hath raised us up together, and made us sit together in heavenly places in Christ Jesus:

God's plan is that the same power that was seen in the 2nd Adam, Jesus Christ, will be seen in the sons of God!

God is serious about His church. He wants us to operate out of His river. We must learn to live and operate out of the river of His Spirit.

Let's look at the rivers in the book of Genesis. It will show us a type and shadow of the river that flows from His throne.

God never intended man to leave Eden. Eden was man's original home. In this paradise, man had access to every blessing, living in unhindered fellowship with God, and the river of God flowed there.

The word Eden means pleasure or delight. There was fellowship with God in this place of pleasure and delight. This was the environment of God. He placed man there. Man did not have to go looking for God.

A river flowed through Eden. Even though man was driven out of the garden, all things have been restored to us through Jesus so we now have access through the blood of Christ.

Genesis 2

8 And the LORD God planted a garden eastward in Eden, and there he put the man whom he had formed.
9 And out of the ground made the LORD God to grow every tree that is pleasant to the sight, and good for food; the tree of life also in the midst of the garden, and the tree of knowledge of good and evil.
10 And a river went out of Eden to water the garden, and from thence it was parted and became into four heads.
11 The name of the first is Pison: that is, it which compasseth the whole land of Havilah, where there is gold;
12 And the gold of that land is good: there are bdellium and the onyx stone.
13 And the name of the second river is Gihon: the same is it that compasseth the whole land of Ethiopia.
14 And the name of the third river is Hiddekel: that is, it which goeth toward the east of Assyria. And the fourth river is the Euphrates.
15 And the LORD God took the man and put him into the garden of Eden to dress it and to keep it.

The river parted into 4 heads. The number 4 represents God's creative power in the earth. Let's look at each of the four rivers.

The Four Rivers Named

1. The name of the first river is Pison:

Pison is translated as increase. According to Strong's Concordance, it means to spread, to grow up, to grow fat, to scatter, to disperse. It also means to spring about, to frisk, to act proudly.

Pison implies the idea of spreading and increasing. Dispersive is the word. Since dispersive is the thought behind the meaning of the name of the first river, we can see a spiritual principle.

God's first and foremost priority is the thought of having His Spirit flow through us to the world. We must be saturated with the Spirit of God in order to disperse it to the world.

This must be our first priority after receiving God's Spirit. Jesus said from our innermost being shall flow rivers of living water so we can have the power we need to be His witness.

This also implies fruitfulness, expansion and a constant flow of life and blessings.

The Bible says gold if found there. Gold represents His deity and His glory. This is also the river releases prosperity and frees us from curses of lack and poverty.

The Pison was in the land of Havilah, meaning circular. It comes from the Hebrew word chuwl, which means to twist or whirl in a circular manner as in dancing. It also means to writhe in pain or fear, to wait, to bring forth, to travail (with pain), to tremble, trust or wait carefully.

We are told to pray always without ceasing. Therefore, Pison represents the river of intercession. These waters wash away barrenness, hopelessness, containment, and non-productivity.

They are healing waters that overthrow thrones of iniquity and poverty.

2. The name of the second river is the Gihon.

Gihon means "bursting forth" – to gush forth as water, to break forth, to bring forth as a woman in labor, to burst forth, to take out. It also means to be opened or to increase.

Gihon implies that what has been shut up, closed off, restricted, confined, not able to be free, or that which was imprisoned will now break out.

Gihon represents breaking out of old structures to experience the breakthrough!

- ➢ Break out of prison structures!
- ➢ Break out of fear!
- ➢ Break out of guilt!

> Break out of hope deferred.

We are not meant to be imprisoned or confined in any way. Jesus Christ did not die for us to be in bondage or confined by anyone, at any time, for any reason! Burst forth!

We were not meant to merely trickle forth the Spirit of God. We must be filled with the Spirit so that it overflows and bursts forth everywhere we go!

This river produces breakout for breakthrough! It is time for the breakthrough generation to rise up

3.The name of the third river is Hiddekel.

It is also known as the Tigris River. Hiddekel means rapid likes the run of a swift horse, not a slow gallop. It does not imply the

gentle sound of force of a quiet stream. Therefore, this river represents warfare. The warfare mantle prepares us and empowers us for the battles ahead.

It goes toward the east. The glory of the Lord came from the east. Therefore, this river moves us from glory to glory.

This river requires rapid levels of maturity and growth. When praying and working with the Spirit of

God, it is the thought of His doing a quick work – the work that God desires to accomplish both in us and through us. We must allow the Spirit of God to flow through us in warfare to enforce the victory our Lord has already won.

4. The fourth river is named the Euphrates.

It means to break forth like a rushing river. It also means to be fertile, to be fruitful and to increase. The idea is that this river is able to carry barges with goods for others. Therefore, it represents evangelism and healing. This river is not only for our own personal growth but also for our family, our ministry, our church, our city and for the nations. It was the largest and longest river.

In John chapter 4:3-30, we read a story about a woman from the town of Samaria. Her encounter with Jesus not only changed her life but the life of those she came in contact with.

She was the most unlikely person to have such a life-changing encounter but Jesus opened the well that was in her and her to the father, then made her a supplier of the water of life.

Notice what Jesus said in John 4

14 But whosoever drinketh of the water that I shall give him shall never thirst, but the water that I shall give him shall be in him a well of water springing up into everlasting life. Notice, Jesus said the water that shall in "in him."

These rivers are within us! John 7

37 In the last day, that great day of the feast, Jesus stood and cried saying, If any man thirst, let him come unto me, and drink.
38 He that believeth on me, as the scripture hath said, out of his belly shall flow rivers of living water.
39 (But this spake he of the Spirit, which they that believe on him should receive: for the Holy Ghost was not yet given; because that Jesus was not yet glorified.)

This statement confirms that the rivers are in us. Notice the word rivers is plural.

Even as the Samaritan woman went without fear and told everyone to "come see a man," she became not only one who would release living water but she became an entry point for others to come into the kingdom.

God is looking for a man or woman who is willing to be an entry point for Him to release the waters of life - the rivers that flow from His Spirit, to be healing for the nations.

Let God open your well, connect you to Father and make you a supplier of the river of life.

Jesus was speaking of Holy Spirit who was poured out of the day of Pentecost. When we pray in the Spirit, in our heavenly language of tongues, we release rivers of living water. We release rivers of intercession, breakthrough, warfare, healing, and evangelism. This is how we prophesy from the river. Each river has its own sound. The river of intercession will have a different sound than the river of warfare or the river of healing.

> *God is looking for a man or woman who is willing to be an entry point for Him to release the waters of life - the rivers that flow from His Spirit, to be healing for the nations.*

The Lord your God is mighty! His voice through you is powerful! Release it everywhere!

Ezekiel 47

> **1** Afterward he brought me again unto the door of the house; and, behold, waters issued out from under the threshold of the house eastward: for the forefront of the house stood toward the east, and the waters came down from under from the right side of the house, at the south side of the altar.
> **7** Now when I had returned, behold, at the bank of the river were very many trees on the one side and on the other.
> **8** Then said he unto me, these waters issue out toward the east country, and go down into the desert, and go into the sea: which being brought forth into the sea, the waters shall be healed.
> **9** And it shall come to pass, that everything that liveth, which moveth, whithersoever the rivers shall come, shall live: and there shall be a very great multitude of fish because these waters shall come thither: for they shall be healed, and everything shall live whither the river cometh.

This is a season of God's immeasurable dimensions. Up until now, we have only known measures of this river. There has been a release of the river that has been line upon line and precept upon precept. But it has still been measurable.

God wants a people who will give themselves totally to Him, who can love in immeasurable dimensions of His Glory and His Spirit until there are waters to swim in.

You can measure water in a glass, in a tank, in a pool or in a lake but oceans cannot be measured.

Let's allow the river of God to flow from us as we pray and prophesy from each river.

Let the prophetic rivers flow to each sphere of our society:

- Government
- Religion
- Financial
- Education
- Family
- Arts and entertainment
- Science and technology
- Media
- Healthcare

Position yourself at the throne of God and let the rivers flow from your innermost being. Let these rivers be for the healing of the nations.

Prophecy from the river with waters of intercession for you and for your family, rivers of breakthrough where there has been resistance, rivers of warfare for difficult situations and rivers of healing for the nation and evangelism for the lost.

These latter times will be marked by an outpouring of God's Spirit on all flesh - not only a few men at selected times for specific duties but all men.

In the Old Testament, Holy Spirit was not poured out on all flesh.

Instead, certain men were filled with the Spirit at certain times and only for certain duties. It was rather selective.

A few examples are:

- Joseph was filled with the Spirit of God (Genesis 41:38)

- The craftsmen who built the tabernacle were filled with the Spirit of God (Exodus 31:3)

- Joshua was filled with the Spirit of God (Numbers 27:18)

- Judges were filled with the Spirit of God (Judges 3:10, 6:34, 11:29, 13:25)

- Even Saul was filled with the Spirit of God (1 Samuel 10:9-10)

- David was filled with the Spirit of God (1 Samuel 16:13)

- But Holy Spirit was not poured out on all flesh.

Acts 1
8 But ye shall receive power, after that the Holy Ghost is come upon you: and ye shall be witnesses unto me both in Jerusalem, and in all Judaea, and in Samaria, and unto the uttermost part of the earth.

Acts 2
16 But this is that which was spoken by the prophet Joel;
17 And it shall come to pass in the last days, saith God, I will pour out of my Spirit upon all flesh: and your sons and your

daughters shall prophesy, and your young men shall see visions, and your old men shall dream dreams:
18 And on my servants and on my handmaidens, I will pour out in those days of my Spirit, and they shall prophesy

Jude 20-21
20 But ye, beloved, building up yourselves on your most holy faith, praying in the Holy Ghost,
21 Keep yourselves in the love of God, looking for the mercy of our Lord Jesus Christ unto eternal life.

It is time to be filled with His Spirit, let His river flow and prophecy from the river.

ACTION

Ask the Lord to give you a prophetic word to release through prayer, song or dance for each one of the rivers as you intercede and pray in the Spirit.

4 UNLOCKING THE SOUNDS OF GOD

God is a God of sound. The body of Christ must awaken to the sounds of God's prophetic dimensions in worship.

Prophetic dimensions in worship help you gain the wisdom you need to prosper. Prophetic mantles are being released for a new dimension in prophetic worship. Ask Holy Spirit to tune your ears to hear. Stop and ask right now!

Ask for the revelation you need to move forward. Stop and ask right now!

Prophetic people must see and hear a new Prophetic release.

That's how we hear the voice of God.

We allow Him room to speak. Then He will release what's needed.

- Welcome the prophetic into your life, into the atmosphere.

- Ask for new strategies!

- Ask for new measures of wisdom!

- Ask for the right sound to create an atmosphere for victory!

- New songs break old cycles. What and who are you listening to?

It makes sense that sounds would be important because Lucifer was the carrier of the sound. The very things that he was created and purposed to do, God now uses as a weapon against him.

We cannot be surrounded with old sounds. We must have His new sounds to break old cycles or we will stay in a wilderness place.

The prophetic sound will break us through into the new!

It is easy to get used to the familiar – familiar songs, familiar sounds. The prophetic dimension in worship will awaken us to hear His voice, it will release healing, restoration, transformation and revelation necessary to change nations.

There are sounds in heaven that God wants to release in the earth realm. The body of Chris is arising to new levels of kingdom worship that releases the government of God in the earth.

Sounds are everywhere. Where you are depending on what you hear. If you are at the zoo, you hear the sound of animals. If you are at a sporting event, you will hear the sounds of shouts. If you are in the secret place, you will hear the voice of God.

Sounds of Heaven

Psalm 150
> **1** Praise ye the LORD. Praise God in his sanctuary: praise him in the firmament of his power.
> **2** Praise him for his mighty acts: praise him according to his excellent greatness.
> **3** Praise him with the sound of the trumpet: praise him with the psaltery and harp.
> **4** Praise him with the timbrel and dance: praise him with stringed instruments and organs.
> **5** Praise him upon the loud cymbals: praise him upon the high- sounding cymbals.
> **6** Let everything that hath breath praise the LORD. Praise ye the LORD.

Have everyone raise hands and say who God is to them. My healer, my Strength, Jehovah Shalom, etc.

Psalm 148
> **1** Praise ye the LORD. Praise ye the LORD from the heavens: praise him in the heights.
> **2** Praise ye him, all his angels: praise ye him, all his hosts.
> **3** Praise ye him, sun and moon: praise him, all ye stars of light.

4 Praise him, ye heavens of heavens, and ye waters that be above the heavens.
5 Let them praise the name of the LORD: for he commanded, and they were created.
6 He hath also established them for ever and ever: he hath made a decree which shall not pass.
7 Praise the LORD from the earth, ye dragons, and all deeps:
8 Fire, and hail; snow, and vapor; stormy wind fulfilling his word:
9 Mountains, and all hills; fruitful trees, and all cedars:
10 Beasts, and all cattle; creeping things, and flying fowl:
11 Kings of the earth, and all people; princes, and all judges of the earth:
12 Both young men, and maidens; old men, and children:
13 Let them praise the name of the LORD: for his name alone is excellent; his glory is above the earth and heaven.
14 He also exalteth the horn of his people, the praise of all his saints; even of the children of Israel, a people near unto him. Praise ye the LORD.

All of creation worships God with sound, from the howling of the winds, the chirping of birds, the barking of dogs, the meows of cats, the sound of rain on a rooftop, the waves of the ocean.

The word praise is the Hebrew word Halal, which means to shine, to boast and to act clamorously foolish before the Lord!

In verse 14, the first mention of praise is the only word in that Psalm that means to sing. It is the word tehilla.

The sound of His presence produces movement, thankfulness, and sound.

Many words for praise involve sound and /or movement of the body. For example:

Yadah means to hold out) the hand; physically, to throw (a stone, an arrow) at or away; especially to revere or worship (with extended hands); intensively, to bemoan (by wringing the hands): --to make a confession of praise, to give) thanks

Towdah means an extension of the hand, adoration; specifically, a choir of worshippers: to give a sacrifice of praise or thanks offering

Barak means to kneel, to bless God as an act of adoration, to praise, salute or thank

Shabach means to address in a loud tone, to glory, praise, to triumph.

There are several words for shout in the Old Testament. Here are three of the words.
- Rua is a battle cry.
- Teruah means to sound the alarm.

- Shabach means to address with a loud tone, to command, to triumph.

He is The God of Sound

All of creation worships God with sound, from the howling of the winds, the chirping of birds, the barking of dogs, the meows of cats, the sound of rain on a rooftop, the waves of the ocean. If you have ever heard a tornado or a hurricane, you will know that they produce a ferocious sound.

The Bible tells us that around His throne there are lightening, thunder, colors we have not seen, sounds we have not heard.

Revelation 5

11 And I beheld, and I heard the voice of many angels round about the throne and the beasts and the elders: and the number of them was ten thousand times ten thousand, and thousands of thousands;
12 Saying with a loud voice, Worthy is the Lamb that was slain to receive power, and riches, and wisdom, and strength, and honor, and glory, and blessing.

Singing in one accord can change lives. When sounds go out into the atmosphere, the sounds can bring unity that sets the atmosphere for His presence.

When the enemy came against Jehoshaphat, it was the sight, sound, and heart of corporate worship that released the glory of God and brought deliverance to everyone.

2 Chronicles 5

> *13 It came even to pass, as the trumpeters and singers were as one, to make one sound to be heard in praising and thanking the LORD; and when they lifted up their voice with the trumpets and cymbals and instruments of musick, and praised the LORD, saying, For he is good; for his mercy endureth forever: that then the house was filled with a cloud; even the house of the LORD;*
> *14 So that the priests could not stand to minister by reason of the cloud: for the glory of the LORD had filled the house of God.*

Dancing in one accord can have the same effect. When ministry takes place with the same heart and the same focus, an agreement forms in the spirit realm and aligns with what happens in heaven. As in heaven, so in earth. Then the angels join us in the worship of our King.

The universe is filled with sound. Every day, scientist listen for sounds in the plates of the earth so they can warn us of upcoming earthquakes.

It has been reported that as they were listening, they heard sounds coming from the rocks and from the plates of the earth.

It is well known that dolphins and whales have a distinct language. It has been researched that our DNA is actually musical decoding. Researchers took the cell of a mouse and decoded it and it replayed to them as music. The sounds of crickets have been recorded and reprogrammed and have been recorded as producing a beautiful, harmonious sound.

Cancer cells have been studied. It was discovered that the decoding of cancer cells is an exact match to the funeral march written by Chopin.

He was playing what was in him. He died of this disease. This was later discovered, as they did not understand it to be cancer at the time.

Healing and deliverance can come from worshippers, musicians, and dancers. We can release the life-giving sounds of God!

Sounds from Heaven Will Invade Earth

Those with ears to hear will hear the sound and bring the sounds from heaven to earth.

God wants us to come into agreement with the sound.

The word symphony comes from a word that means two coming into agreement. We can choose to come into agreement with the sound or reject it. When we choose to receive it, we become an instrument of heavens sound. The earth echoes the sounds of heaven.

Romans 8
19 For the earnest expectation of the creature waiteth
for the manifestation of the sons of God.

It makes sense that sound would be important because Lucifer was the carrier of the sound. He was an instrument. He was the sound.

The very thing that he was created and purposed to do, God now uses as a weapon against him.

Ezekiel 28 reads as follows:
> **13** Thou hast been in Eden the garden of God; every precious stone was thy covering, the sardius, topaz, and the diamond, the beryl, the onyx, and the jasper, the sapphire, the emerald, and the carbuncle, and gold: the workmanship of thy tabrets and of thy pipes was prepared in thee in the day that thou was created.
> **14** Thou art the anointed cherub that covereth; and I have set thee so: thou wast upon the holy mountain of God; thou hast walked up and down in the midst of the stones of fire.
> **15** Thou wast perfect in thy ways from the day that thou wast created, till iniquity was found in thee.
> **16** By the multitude of thy merchandise, they have filled the midst of thee with violence, and thou hast sinned: therefore, I will cast thee as profane out of the mountain of God: and I will destroy thee, O covering cherub, from the midst of the stones of fire.
> **17** Thine heart was lifted up because of thy beauty, thou hast corrupted thy wisdom by reason of thy brightness: I will cast thee to the ground, I will lay thee before kings, that they may behold thee.
> **18** Thou hast defiled thy sanctuaries by the multitude of thine iniquities, by the iniquity of thy traffick; therefore, will I bring forth a fire from the midst of thee, it shall devour thee, and I will bring thee to ashes upon the earth in the sight of all them that behold thee.
> **19** All they that know thee among the people shall be astonished at thee: thou shalt be a terror, and never shalt thou be anymore.

Isaiah 14

12 How art thou fallen from heaven, O Lucifer, son of the morning! how art thou cut down to the ground, which didst weakens the nations!

13 For thou hast said in thine heart, I will ascend into heaven, I will exalt my throne above the stars of God: I will sit also upon the mount of the congregation, in the sides of the north:

14 I will ascend above the heights of the clouds; I will be like the most High.

15 Yet thou shalt be brought down to hell, to the sides of the pit.

16 They that see thee shall narrowly look upon thee, and consider thee, saying, Is this the man that made the earth to tremble, that did shake kingdoms;

The words of Jesus from Luke 10

18 I saw Satan fall like lightning from heaven.

19 I have given you the authority to trample on snakes and scorpions and to overcome all the power of the enemy; nothing will harm you.

Now we are the sounds of God! The privilege is ours to be the sounds of God in the earth as we reflect the sounds coming from the heavens. When heavenly music is birthed and released into the earth and we sing and come into agreement, we become His voice, His sound in the earth.

Zephaniah 3

17 God in the midst of thee is mighty.

We are His holy habitation, His tabernacle where 24-hour worship is to take place. Therefore, we become instruments to release His sound. Now is the time for the sound of the kingdom advancing!

Jesus was the sound of God released to redeem the earth to the Father.

> *Jesus was the sound of God released to redeem the earth to the Father.*

The day of Pentecost was the sound of heaven released into the earth like as unto a mighty rushing wind. This was no quiet event!

Matthew 28

31 And he shall send his angels with a great sound of a trumpet, and they shall gather together his elect from the four winds, from one end of heaven to the other.

We are called to be the Gods covenant people who release the sounds of heaven as God's prophetic authority so others can experience His presence and have an encounter with the living God.

The Bible is Filled with Sound!

1 Kings 18:41 mentions the sound of an 'abundance of rain."

1 Chronicles 15 mentions songs and sounds.
> **27***And David was clothed with a robe of fine linen, and all the Levites that bare the ark, and the singers, and Chenaniah the master of the song with the singers: David also had upon him an ephod of linen.*
> **28***Thus all Israel brought up the ark of the covenant of the LORD with shouting, and with sound of the cornet, and with trumpets, and with cymbals, making a noise with psalteries and harps.*
> **29***And it came to pass, as the ark of the covenant of the LORD came to the city of David, that Michal the daughter of Saul looking out at a window saw king David dancing and playing: and she despised him in her heart.*

The human voice consists of sound made by a human being using the vocal folds for talking, singing, laughing, crying, screaming, etc.

The human voice is specifically that part of human sound production in which the vocal folds (vocal cords) are the primary sound source.

A sound is a form of energy. Try this test. Put your index and middle finger on your neck. Say the word "Aah" as loud as you can. Then try it as soft as you can. You not only hear a sound, but you can feel a movement inside your throat. When you say, "Aah", your vocal cords vibrate. That means they move quickly back and forth. As your vocal cords vibrate they produce sound.

The enemy wants to keep you fearful and quiet but you are a sound instrument. When you get a physical exam, the doctors ask to listen to your heart! Your heart has a sound! They can also hear blood as it rushes through your veins! Your nose can make a sound if you're breathing is heavy. Your hands make a sound when you clap them. Bare feet can even make a sound, depending on the surface of the ground or the speed of the steps.

God spoke all things into existence and all things are held together by the word of His power, by the sound of His voice.

Hebrews 1

3 Who being the brightness of his glory, and the express image of his person, and upholding all things by the word of his power, when he had by himself purged our sins, sat down on the right hand of the Majesty on high;

His voice sustains all matter! His voice walks!

Genesis 3

8 And they heard the voice of the LORD God walking in the garden in the cool of the day: and Adam and his wife hid themselves from the presence of the LORD God amongst the trees of the garden.

The word walking can be translated as to whirl.

His voice heals.

Exodus 15

26 And said, If thou wilt diligently hearken to the voice of the LORD thy God, and wilt do that which is right in his sight, and wilt give ear to his commandments and keep all his statutes, I will put none of these diseases upon thee, which

I have brought upon the Egyptians: for I am the LORD that healeth thee.

1 Kings 19

11 And he said, Go forth, and stand upon the mount before the LORD. And, behold, the LORD passed by, and a great and strong wind rent the mountains, and brake in pieces the rocks before the LORD; but the LORD was not in the wind: and after the wind an earthquake; but the LORD was not in the earthquake:

12 And after the earthquake a fire; but the LORD was not in the fire: and after the fire a still small voice.

Psalm 29

3 The voice of the LORD is upon the waters: the God of glory thundereth: the LORD is upon many waters.

4 The voice of the LORD is powerful; the voice of the LORD is full of majesty.

5 The voice of the LORD breaketh the cedars; yea, the LORD breaketh the cedars of Lebanon.

6 He maketh them also to skip like a calf; Lebanon and Sirion like a young unicorn.

7 The voice of the LORD divideth the flames of fire.

8 The voice of the LORD shaketh the wilderness; the LORD shaketh the wilderness of Kadesh.

9 The voice of the LORD maketh the hinds to calve, and discovereth the forests: and in his temple doth every one speak of his glory.

The gifts of the Spirit are mentioned in 1 Corinthians 12. Of the nine gifts listed there, five of the gifts require the release of a sound.

1Corinthians 12

8 For to one is given by the Spirit the word of wisdom. to another the word of knowledge by the same Spirit;
9 To another faith by the same Spirit. to another the gifts of healing by the same Spirit;
10 To another the working of miracles. to another prophecy. to another discerning of spirits. to another divers kind of tongues. to another the interpretation of tongues...

There are sounds for each supernatural manifestation:

Joy has a sound.

Jeremiah 33

11 The voice of joy, and the voice of gladness, the voice of the bridegroom, and the voice of the bride, the voice of them that shall say, Praise the LORD of hosts: for the LORD is good; for his mercy endureth forever: and of them that shall bring the sacrifice of praise into the house of the LORD. For I will cause to return the captivity of the land, as at the first, saith the LORD.

Rejoicing and salvation have a sound.

Psalm 118
>15 The voice of rejoicing and salvation is in the tabernacles of the righteous: the right hand of the LORD doeth valiantly.

Repentance has a sound.

Joel 2
>12 Therefore also now, saith the LORD, turn ye even to me with all your heart, and with fasting, and with weeping, and with mourning:

Even forgiveness, hurt, frustration each have their sound.

Faith has a sound!

Dancing has a sound!

Luke 15
>25 Now his elder son was in the field: and as he came and drew nigh to the house, he heard musick and dancing.

Creation Sounds

Romans 8
>19 For the earnest expectation of the creature waiteth for the manifestation of the sons of God.
>22 For we know that the whole creation groaneth and travaileth in pain together until now.

Creation even makes a sound. It is a sound of groaning and travail, waiting for us to come in agreement with who God says we are!

Our Sounds

I have discovered that many dancers do not understand the power of their own voice. We must each learn to lift up our voice to the Lord and make a joyful noise in prayer, praise, worship, and intercession.

> **23** And not only they but ourselves also, which have the first fruits of the Spirit, even we ourselves groan within ourselves, waiting for the adoption, to wit, the redemption of our body.

What is the sound of your destiny?

JUBILEE

Leviticus 25
> **9** Then shalt thou cause the trumpet of the jubilee to sound on the tenth day of the seventh month, in the day of atonement shall ye make the trumpet sound throughout all your land.

REPENTANCE

Isaiah 58

1 Cry aloud, spare not, lift up thy voice like a trumpet, and shew my people their transgression, and the house of Jacob their sins.

WARFARE

Numbers 10

9 And if ye go to war in your land against the enemy that oppresseth you, then ye shall blow an alarm with the trumpets; and ye shall be remembered before the LORD your God, and ye shall be saved from your enemies.

WORSHIP

Exodus 28

35 And it shall be upon Aaron to minister: and his sound shall be heard when he goeth in unto the holy place before the LORD, and when he cometh out, that he die not.

VICTORY

Joshua 6

5 And it shall come to pass, that when they make a long blast with the ram's horn, and when ye hear the sound of the trumpet, all the people shall shout with a great shout;

and the wall of the city shall fall down flat, and the people shall ascend up every man straight before him.

2 Samuel 5

24 And let it be, when thou hearest the sound of a going (steps) in the tops of the mulberry trees, that then thou shalt bestir thyself: for then shall the LORD go out before thee, to smite the host of the Philistines.

GOD'S PRESENCE

2 Samuel 16

13 And it was so, that when they that bare the ark of the LORD had gone six paces, he sacrificed oxen and fatlings.
14 And David danced before the LORD with all his might, and David was girded with a linen ephod.
15 So David and all the house of Israel brought up the ark of the LORD with shouting, and with the sound of the trumpet.
16 And as the ark of the LORD came into the city of David, Michal Saul's daughter looked through a window, and saw king David leaping and dancing before the LORD; and she despised him in her heart.

DECLARING THE KING

2 Samuel 15

10 But Absalom sent spies throughout all the tribes of Israel, saying, As soon as ye hear the sound of the trumpet, then ye shall say, Absalom reigneth in Hebron.

***1 Kings 1* (David made Solomon King)**
>40 And all the people came up after him, and the people piped with pipes and rejoiced with great joy so that the earth rent with the sound of them.

PRAISE AND THANKSGIVING

2 Chronicles 5
>13 It came even to pass, as the trumpeters and singers were as one, to make one sound to be heard in praising and thanking the LORD; and when they lifted up their voice with the trumpets and cymbals and instruments of musick, and praised the LORD, saying, For he is good; for his mercy endureth for ever: that then the house was filled with a cloud, even the house of the LORD;
>14 So that the priests could not stand to minister by reason of the cloud: for the glory of the LORD had filled the house of God.

GOD ARISES

Psalm 47
>5 God is gone up (ascend) with a shout, the LORD with the SOUND of a trumpet.
>6 Sing praises to God, sing praises: sing praises unto our King, sing praises.

Psalm 77
>16 The waters saw thee, O God, the waters saw thee; they were afraid: the depths also were troubled.

17 The clouds poured out water: the skies sent out a sound: thine arrows also went abroad.
18 The voice of thy thunder was in the heaven: the lightning lightened the world: the earth trembled and shook.
19 Thy way is in the sea, and thy path in the great waters and thy footsteps (LIKE THE SOUND OF HORSES) are not known.

GOD'S PEOPLE

Psalm 89

15 Blessed is the people that know the joyful sound: they shall walk, O LORD, in the light of thy countenance.

THE SOUND OF FAITH

Mark 10

46 And they came to Jericho: and as he went out of Jericho with his disciples and a great number of people, blind Bartimaeus, the son of Timaeus, sat by the highway side begging.

47 And when he heard that it was Jesus of Nazareth, he began to cry out, and say, Jesus, thou Son of David, have mercy on me.

48 And many charged him that he should hold his peace: but he cried the more a great deal, Thou Son of David, have mercy on me.

49 And Jesus stood still and commanded him to be called. And they call the blind man, saying unto him, Be of good comfort, rise; he called thee.

50 And he, casting away his garment, rose, and came to Jesus.

51 And Jesus answered and said unto him, What wilt thou that I should do unto thee? The blind man said unto him, Lord, that I might receive my sight.

52 And Jesus said unto him, Go thy way; thy faith hath made thee whole. And immediately he received his sight and followed Jesus in the way.

- What sounds does God want to unlock in you?
- What sounds does God want to release in the earth?
- What sounds are you making?
- Who is listening?
- What are you saying?
- Are lives being changed by your sound?
- Are nations changing because of your sound?

Whether your sound is one of crying, seeking, searching, calling, watching, waiting, thirst, desperation, preaching or prophecy....you are called to release God's sound!

Focus on listening to what God wants to say, then release it in the earth. Repeat – hear from heaven, release it in the earth.

We cannot depend on old sounds.

We must have new sound to break old cycles or we will be in danger of staying in a wilderness place.

Learn to listen to what Holy Spirit wants to say

2 Kings 3
> **15** But now bring me a minstrel. And it came to pass, when the minstrel played, that the hand of the LORD came upon him.

As the minstrel played, the Spirit of God was released that brought strategy for the victory of the people.

A minstrel is not just one who plays an instrument. A minstrel anointed by God can and will shift atmospheres as they yield to Holy Spirit.

1 Samuel 16:23

Whenever the spirit from God came on Saul, David would take up his lyre and play.

Then relief would come to Saul; he would feel better, and the evil spirit would leave him.

Psalmists are not just those who can sing. David was referred to as the sweet Psalmist of Israel.

> *The function of the worship team is to hear from heaven, say what heaven is saying and prophesy life.*

1 Chronicles 9 tells us that they had daily responsibilities in the temple.
33 And these are the singers, chief of the fathers of the Levites, who remaining in the chambers were free: for they were employed in that work day and night.

The Psalmists actually sang over people to lift the heavy burdens off of the people so they could receive the word of God.

The function of the worship team is to hear from heaven, say what heaven is saying and prophesy life.

- Prophesy destiny!
- Prophesy victory!
- Prophecy the will of God to people - to the nations!

New prophetic songs and sounds can break us through to the new! This is a new season! It is time for new songs!

Isaiah 42:9-10

9 Behold, the former things are come to pass, and new things do I declare: before they spring forth I tell you of them.
10 Sing unto the LORD a new song, and his praise from the end of the earth....

Psalm 33:3

3 Sing unto him a new song;

Psalm 40

3 And he hath put a new song in my mouth, even praise unto our God

Psalm 96

1 O sing unto the LORD a new song

Psalm 98

1 A Psalm. O sing unto the LORD a new song; for he hath done marvelous things: his right hand, and his holy arm, hath gotten him the victory.

Psalm 144

9 I will sing a new song unto thee

Psalm 149

1 Praise ye the LORD. Sing unto the LORD a new song

ACTION

Begin to sing, shout and release your sound into the earth! Ask for songs and dances of joy, victory, jubilee, repentance, warfare, praise and thanksgiving.

5 WORSHIP THAT ESTABLISHES HIS KINGDOM

You are now stepping into destiny that was for you from before the foundations of the earth. God saw you from the time you were in your mother's womb and He has planned every day of your life to fit perfectly into His plan. Each day that you wake up is a new day for you to step into purpose.

There is a new fire on the lampstand that is assembling worshippers from every nation that will create a new atmosphere in the earth realm. The prayer, "Thy kingdom come, thy will be done", is becoming a reality in the earth. Where we see God's will be done, we see His Kingdom is established.

God has been shifting us out of old structures, even old worship structures. This is the season for a new administration in worship.

I believe we are in a time when we will see the victorious church arise.

The worship of the victorious church has to do with who will win the war for the atmosphere and territory.

Matt 16
> **13** When Jesus came into the coasts of Caesarea Philippi, he asked his disciples, saying, Whom do men say that I the Son of man am?
> **14** And they said Some say that thou art John the Baptist: some, Elias; and others, Jeremias, or one of the prophets.
> **15** He saith unto them, But whom say ye that I am?
> **16** And Simon Peter answered and said, Thou art the Christ, the Son of the living God.
> **17** And Jesus answered and said unto him, Blessed art thou, Simon Barona: for flesh and blood hath not revealed it unto thee, but my Father which is in heaven.
> **18** And I say also unto thee, That thou art Peter, and upon this rock, I will build my church; and the gates of hell shall not prevail against it.
> **19** And I will give unto thee the keys of the kingdom of heaven: and whatsoever thou shalt bind on earth shall be bound in heaven: and whatsoever thou shalt loose on earth shall be loosed in heaven.

Worship is a key given to us for the establishment of His Kingdom.

In verse 18, the word church is not a religious term. The word is more accurately translated as ecclesia. It is a governmental term meaning the called out ones. It was used to refer to a senate - those chosen by the government (cabinet members) to be a governing body.

Their job was to know the mind of the king, (Caesar) - receive his thoughts, his desires, his passion and his intent and then turn it into legislation that can be implemented for the kingdom.

Their job was to stay in close contact with the king.

This ecclesia was trusted with information so critical to the operation of the kingdom, that even hell itself cannot prevail against it.

We are the ecclesia! We are called to operate on another level, unlike the world. We have access to the power of the throne. It is a throne of grace and we must come boldly. We have already passed from death to life and the scripture tells us that we have been given keys of worship to unlock the Kingdom, to take authority, to exercise dominion and to access all of heavens resources.

Worship gives us access to the throne, the governmental seat of authority.

All authority is given to us! His presence, power, and authority are with us because He is with us and He has given us His keys.

Keys represent authority - they represent access. You have no authority in my home so you cannot give the authority to access my home to another person. It belongs to the one who has the keys and the authority to give it. But If I give you the keys to my home, you would then have authority to access it at any time.

God, who has all authority has given us the keys and the anointing of His authority to demonstrate Him in the earth.

Keys cannot be substituted with feelings, emotions, wishful thinking or manipulation. You can fast and pray outside of my home all night but without the key, the door will not open. You need a key.

Our mandate is to know the times and the seasons of God for worship in these last days so we can unlock the resources of heaven and release the prophetic destiny God has for us.

- Ecclesia! Let's awake to new dimensions in worship.
- Arise to new levels of worship.
- Advance in worship.
- Penetrate the darkness through worship.
- Breakthrough old structures with worship.
- Transform hearts and lives through worship.

Jesus is speaking to His disciples in Matthew 28:
17 And when they saw him, they worshipped him:
18 And Jesus came and spake unto them, saying, All power is given unto me in heaven and in earth.

Once they worshipped, He began to speak to them about power and authority.

Authority means lawful rights and jurisdiction, ability, privilege, force, capacity, delegated influence, liberty, power, right, and strength.

Worship is not only about intimacy, worship is a governmental force of God's kingdom in the earth.

That's why the enemy would like to keep God's people in the arena of our emotions. But God has given this ecclesia power and worship releases a governmental authority beyond the realm of our emotions.

This is the season, the hour, the day, the time of the restored ecclesia.

The delegated authority given in His name will advance the key of binding and loosing in the ecclesia of God through worship.

With this authority will come an awaking for restoration, healing with be released, we will see the transfer of wealth, the harvest will come in and revelation will come that will change nations.

As the ekklesia represents God's government in the earth, our worship is to facilitate the government of God as He enthrones Himself on our praises.

Psalm 22:3 tells us that God inhabits our praises. To inhabit is the word yashah, meaning He comes to dwell and to sit down as a judge. So, God will come to enthrone Himself as judge in our praises.

When we tehilla (sing), God manifests His power.

Our cry should be, "Lord, you are enthroned! Manifest the power of your throne on the praises of His people."

So, it is in the midst of the praises of the ecclesia where God sits down as judge, thus bringing His governmental process to the earth realm.

That is how we yield ourselves to the purposes of God in worship. We don't always associate authority with worship.

We think intimacy, but again, both of these words are associated with worship. He wants us to rule in the midst of our enemies through worship.

Let's look at the Word of God to see some examples.

1. On the day of His triumphal entry, the crowds waved palm branches and threw their coats before King Jesus as he entered Jerusalem riding on a donkey. They had no idea that their praises enthroned Him into His governmental position as King in a new way. He had entered Jerusalem before but on this day, He walked into the temple, took up His kingly authority and began to drive out the money changers.

2. *Psalm 149*

> **6** Let the high praises of God be in their mouth, and a two-edged sword in their hand; WHY?
> **7** To execute vengeance upon the heathen, and punishments upon the people;
> **8** To bind their kings with chains, and their nobles with fetters of iron;
> **9** To execute upon them the judgment written: this honour have ALL his saints. Praise ye the LORD.

Here is what this looks like. Picture a courtroom. There is a judge and someone has committed a crime. The judge pronounces judgment. But the person who committed the crime is not going to joyfully turn himself in so the bailiff comes to execute the judgment (sentence) written by the judge.

God is the judge; the enemy is the convicted criminal and we are the bailiff and this scripture tells us that high praises of God in our mouth execute the judgment written in our constitution:

It is written in 1 John 4
> **4** Ye are of God, little children, and have overcome them because greater is he that is in you, than he that is in the world. It's written in Isaiah 53 **5** But he was wounded for our transgressions, he was bruised for our iniquities: the chastisement of our peace was upon him, and with his stripes, we are healed.

3. Remember Paul and Silas? Sometimes God is just waiting to hear your sound and then He will manifest His presence! Read Acts 16!

It wasn't until Paul and Silas began to worship while in jail, in a tight place, in a hard place, in a place of opposition that God showed up and shook the earth! God was enthroned on their praises and He came as judge!

They didn't whine and complain. They didn't say, "Pour me, let me call all my friends so they can please feel sorry for me." No! They worshipped and God showed up in power.

Their praise was heard by everyone in the prison and brought revelation to them that pricked their hearts so much that they had to ask, "Sirs, what must I do to be saved?" Acts 16:30

> *As God is enthroned, His presence arrives in full power, you say what He says and exercise His dominion, then you go and change the world.*

This is the worship that must come forth from God's people. Worship that will bring deliverance to entire people groups. Praise is the key to freedom from bondage, oppression, and depression.

As God is enthroned on the praises of His people, our declarations of His Kingdom will confront the powers of darkness and victory is assured.

As God is enthroned, His presence arrives in full power, you say what He says and exercise His dominion, then you go and change the world.

So, our worship on earth must reflect the worship in heaven.

Let's look throughout the book of Revelation. All through the book, we see worship released that enthrones the King and it is in this atmosphere of worship that God begins to launch His acts of authority.

You may recall the apocalyptic events of the book of Revelation but these events are woven together with incredible times of worship.

When John was called up from the Isle of Patmos to a door that opened into heaven, he found himself in the midst of an extraordinary atmosphere of worship.

He was surrounded by the worship of the 24 elders and the four living creatures.

Can you imagine? It was intense, passionate, exuberant - some were crying out to the Lord, others were falling down before Him and others sang with a loud voice. God was in the midst of it all - answering prayers, pronouncing judgment and sending the hosts of heaven into a battle to end the devil's reign.

All in the midst of worship! As it is in heaven, so it must be on earth.

Worship in heaven is extravagant, dynamic, explosive, spontaneous. The atmosphere of heaven is filled with Spirit breathed songs.

The worship in heaven is prophetic.

It becomes prophetic when it makes known the heart of God or the works that God plans to release into the earth. There is nothing traditional or man made about the worship in heaven.

None of man's thoughts about how worship should or should not exist in heaven! The sounds of heaven are not filled with the opinions of man.

If you will notice, they don't sing about themselves or how they feel. We must stop leaning on our own understanding or traditions. Let's move past these into a new understanding of kingdom worship

Revelation 5
9 And they sung a new song.

They sang a new song. New means fresh. They sang, not an old song, but a new, fresh song that sprang forth spontaneously. It was prophetic revelation that birthed the new. It caused them to bow down, stand up, shout, sing, celebrate and even make war. Notice that they just did not sing whatever they wanted to sing. They sang according to the heart of God at the time, depending on what God wanted to do. We must do the same in these days.

Let's look at throne room worship.

In the 4th and 5th chapters of Revelation, we begin to see the order of worship around God's throne.

Throne room worship is continual.

Revelation 4
4 And round about the throne were four and twenty seats: and upon the seats, I saw four and twenty elders sitting, clothed in white raiment; and they had on their heads crowns of gold.
6 about the throne were four beasts full of eyes before and behind.

8 they rest not day and night, saying, Holy, holy, holy, Lord God Almighty, which was, and is, and is to come.

10 The four and twenty elders fall down before him that sat on the throne, and worship him that liveth for ever and ever, and cast their crowns before the throne, saying,

11 Thou art worthy, O Lord, to receive glory and honour and power: for thou hast created all things, and for thy pleasure, they are and were created.

Revelation 5

11 the voice of many angels round about the throne and the beasts and the elders: and the number of them was ten thousand times ten thousand, and thousands of thousands;
12 Saying with a loud voice, Worthy is the Lamb that was slain to receive power, and riches, and wisdom, and strength, and honor, and glory, and blessing.

Worship, prayer, intercession and new songs originate at God's throne. Around His throne, you will hear the singing of new songs and the voice of many angels is heard as we see God in His throne room. The lamb is about to open the seven seals and the trumpets of judgment will be sounded.

In Revelation chapter 7, we see a great multitude from every nation, tribe, and tongue worshipping God.

Revelation 7

9 After this I beheld, and, lo, a great multitude, which no man could number, of all nations, and kindreds, and people, and tongues, stood before the throne, and before the Lamb, clothed with white robes, and palms in their hands;

Following this worship, God releases seven angels to sound seven trumpets which bring forth judgments.

Revelation 8
2 And I saw the seven angels which stood before God, and to them were given seven trumpets.

In Chapter 11, there were great voices in heaven saying:

Revelation 11
15 And the seventh angel sounded; and there were great voices in heaven, saying, The kingdoms of this world are become the kingdoms of our Lord, and of his Christ, and he shall reign forever and ever.

And the 24 elders fall down and worship the Lord.

Revelation 11
16 And the four and twenty elders, which sat before God on their seats, fell upon their faces and worshipped God.

In chapter 14, 144,000 worshippers are singing a new song unto the Lamb.

Revelation 14

3 And they sung as it were a new song before the throne, and before the four beasts, and the elders: and no man could learn that song but the hundred and forty and four thousand, which were redeemed from the earth.

After this, the Lord gives the word to reap the earth.

Revelation 14
16 And he that sat on the cloud thrust in his sickle on the earth, and the earth was reaped.

In chapter 15, those who won the victory over the beast took harps and worshipped before the throne singing the Song of Moses and the song of the Lamb.

Revelation 15
3 And they sing the song of Moses the servant of God, and the song of the Lamb, saying, Great and marvelous are thy works, Lord God Almighty; just and true are thy ways, thou King of saints.

In chapter 16, seven bowls of judgment are poured out in the midst of worship from the very angels who were pouring out the judgment.

Revelation 16
1 And I heard a great voice out of the temple saying to the seven angels, Go your ways, and pour out the vials of the wrath of God upon the earth.

And in chapter 19, there is a thunderous worship service by a great multitude.

Revelation 19
   1 And after these things I heard a great voice of much people in heaven, saying, Alleluia; Salvation, and glory, and honour, and power, unto the Lord our God:

Revelation 19
   11 And I saw heaven opened, and behold a white horse, and he that sat upon him was called Faithful and True, and in righteousness, he doth judge and make war.

Jesus then comes forth leading the army of heaven into the battle of Armageddon. As worship rises, God follows taking action to fulfill His purposes.

God is inviting us to do the same thing - enthrone Him on our praises so that we might participate in the judgment He desires to bring into the earth, thereby releasing His acts of authority.

1. The worship in heaven is continual.

Revelation 4
   8 And says the four beasts had each of them six wings about him, and they were full of eyes within: and they rest not day and night, saying, Holy, holy, holy, Lord God Almighty, which was, and is, and is to come.

2. The worship in heaven is face to face. They fell down before

Him.

Revelation 4

10 The four and twenty elders fall down before him that sat on the throne, and worship him that liveth for ever and ever, and cast their crowns before the throne

3. The worship in heaven is prophetic.

Revelation 5

5 And one of the elders saith unto me, Weep not: behold, the Lion of the tribe of Judah, the Root of David, hath prevailed to open the book, and to loose the seven seals thereof.

Worship can also be prophetic revelation. It becomes prophetic when it makes known the heart of God or the works of God that He plans to release into the earth.

4. Worship in heaven is intercessory.

Revelation 5

8 And when he had taken the book, the four beasts and four and twenty elders fell down before the Lamb, having every one of them harps, and golden vials full of odor's, (incense, meaning to fumigate) which are the earnest prayers (can also be translated worship) of the saints....... As the elders 'worship with their harps, the incense from the bowls rises to intermingle with their worship.

So our worship on earth must reflect the worship in heaven.

David knew that when God was enthroned on the praises of His people, the hand of God would prevail against the enemies of Israel.

So, when God says He is rebuilding the Tabernacle of David, this place where the order of worship was first set in place, He intends to establish His throne on the praises of His people and from that throne, remove veils of darkness from the nations so the fullness of His Kingdom can be released.

Amos 9
> **11** In that day will I raise up the tabernacle of David that is fallen, and close up the breaches thereof; and I will raise up his ruins, and I will build it as in the days of old:
> **12** That they may possess the remnant of Edom, and of all the heathen, which are called by my name, saith the LORD that doeth this.

Possess is the word yaresh, meaning to occupy by driving out previous tenants, and possessing in their place. It means to seize, to rob, to disinherit; also, to expel, to ruin, to cast out, consume, destroy and disinherit

So, our worship will drive out, seize, rob, expel, ruin, cast out, consume, destroy, disinherit and dispossess the works of darkness.

We are to occupy and take possession all that has been left behind in the nations by building a tabernacle, habitation for the presence of the
Lord as we enthrone Him in our worship.

We see this again in Acts 15

16 After this I will return, and will build again the tabernacle of David, which is fallen down; and I will build again the ruins thereof, and I will set it up:
17 That the residue of men might seek after the Lord, and all the Gentiles, upon whom my name is called, saith the Lord, who doeth all these things.

We are living in those days.

Matthew 11
12 And from the days of John the Baptist until now the Kingdom of Heaven suffers violence, and the violent take it by force.

It is not about forceful men with natural weapons. It is about being violent or forceful in worship. It is about being a passionate worshipper, desperate for God. It is about our desire to advance the Kingdom of God so that others may experience the same relationship with Jesus - the Christ that we experience.

The violent, strong, vigorous, earnest, fervent, zealous worshipping warriors are arising to seize and advance the kingdom through prophetic dimensions in worship. The reigning church is rising up!

This is the heart of the end-time worship movement.

ACTION

Begin to join the worship in heaven by saying, Holy, Holy, Holy. As God comes to enthrone Himself on your praise, partner with Him in intercession, worship, prayer, and praise to possess your territory and establish His kingdom.

6 BUILDING PROPHETIC WORSHIP ALTARS

We must be living examples of worship. God wants you to take His land back and take His people back. Worship altars will accomplish that.

Egypt represents the world that we live in and the bondage that comes with not serving God.

If we look at history, God's desire for Israel was that they would be free from Egypt to worship Him without constraint, thus the story of Exodus.

That is still His desire for us.

As He told Pharaoh, let my people go so they can worship me. Worship is the central affirmation of God in our lives, above everything else, more important than anything else.

God is looking for a people who will build altars of worship…individual altars, as well as family, city, and nations.

Why were altars so important? If altars were so important to God in the Old Testament, then why don't we build and worship at altars today?

Most people consider the altar to be the front of our church. Yet, this is not really the same type of altar in which Abraham worshipped. Reading through Genesis, you will see that Abraham often built altars to worship the Lord.

What is an altar? An altar is a place of worship where we offer something to God. An altar is a place that keeps God as the main focus of one's life.

So, altars are about worship.

Altars are mentioned some 400 times in the Bible. The Hebrew word for altar is mizbeach, meaning a slaughter place. A blood sacrifice was required. So, an altar is also a place of sacrifice.

Why build an altar? An altar is the meeting place between the physical and the spiritual. It is the place where people go to commune with God.

God expects you to build the altar. He wants you to prepare a place, where the two of you can meet. The building of the altar is a matter of your own choice, your own will and it is your responsibility. It's not enough just to be where the altars are being built. You must build your own.

The altar is where the physical contacts the spiritual and when God desires to do a new work, he looks for people who are passionate in worship, willing to build new altars. People also build altars of worship to the devil.

ABRAHAM – Genesis 12

7 And the LORD appeared unto Abram, and said, Unto thy seed will I give this land: and there built he an altar unto the LORD, who appeared unto him.

The worship of Abraham was not tied to a location. It formed a central part to the prophetic progress of his life. Wherever he traveled he built an altar.

Genesis 13

18 Then Abram removed his tent, and came and dwelt in the plain of Mamre, which is in Hebron, and built there an altar unto the LORD.

Abraham was always moving, always worshipping! That must be our testimony as well.

His most testing experience in life required the building of an altar.

Genesis 22

5 I and the lad will go yonder and worship and come again to you.
9 When they reached the place God had told him about, Abraham built an altar there and arranged wood on it. He bound his son Isaac and laid him on the altar, on top of the wood.

I find it very interesting that Abraham did not have with him the things we associate with worship in many of our churches today. He did not have his favorite worship leader there to sing his favorite song, he did not have a full worship team to lead him. He had no iPad, iPod or CD to play his favorite song. He had no radio, no television. Abraham only had his heart.

As Abraham lifted his hand to slay Issac, the angel appeared and called his name..." Abraham, Abraham." Abraham responded, "HERE AM I."

The calling of his name was not the same as a teacher who calls names of the students in a classroom and the students answer, "Here." It was a call from God, therefore it required a response much deeper than the answer a student gives in a classroom.

Here am I is the word Hineni. It is the ultimate form of worship because it means here am I, one hundred percent - body, soul, spirit and every part of who I am.

Hineni means you are drawing the line, no questions asked. It means whatever the Lord asks of you, your response is Hineni. It is complete submission to the will of God. Hineni is true worship. It is complete obedience. There is no worship without obedience.

The altar of worship is not a place, it's a lifestyle! This is God's call to you and me. We are not called to more church meetings or more religious programs, but to a personal, transforming encounter with his presence.

Some people do not need more counseling, preaching or even deliverance. They need to see Jesus and have an encounter with Him. They need to meet him at an altar, a humble altar built from the rubble of our brokenness and pain, our frustration and fear.

At that place, He comes in sovereign power to set the captives free!

It has been said of Abraham that his paths could be traced by the altars he built.

Can someone trace your paths or the paths of your nation by your altars of worship?

Let's look at Abraham's altars. They are prophetic signposts that show us how He walked with God.

First, we are all familiar with Abraham's commission from God.

Genesis 12
1 Now the LORD had said unto Abram, Get thee out of thy country, and from thy kindred, and from thy father's house, unto a land that I will shew thee:
2 And I will make of thee a great nation, and I will bless thee, and make thy name great, and thou shalt be a blessing:
3 And I will bless them that bless thee, and curse him that curseth thee: and in thee shall all families of the earth be blessed.
4 So Abram departed, as the LORD had spoken unto him...

7 And the LORD appeared unto Abram, and said, Unto thy seed will I give this land: and there built he an altar unto the LORD, who appeared unto him.
8 And he removed from thence unto a mountain on the east of Bethel, and pitched his tent, having Bethel on the west, and Hai on the east: and there he built an altar unto the LORD, and called upon the name of the LORD.

Abraham built altars to God based on the prophetic word and the promises of God even before he saw them come to pass.

What has God promised you?

After his sojourn in Egypt, (he was there because of the famine) Abraham came back to the altar site near Bethel.

Genesis 13

3 And he went on his journeys from the south even to Bethel, unto the place where his tent had been at the beginning, between Bethel and Hai;
4 Unto the place of the altar, which he had made there at the first: and there Abram called on the name of the LORD.

Further, when he and Lot separated and Abram moved to the region of Hebron.

Genesis 13
> *18 Then Abram removed his tent, and came and dwelt in the plain of Mamre, which is in Hebron, and built there an altar unto the LORD.*

But he made mistakes in two incidents involving Sarah. The first incident was with Pharaoh while in Egypt (Gen. 12); and the next, about twenty years later, an identical situation when he practiced deception with Abimelech (Gen. 20).

When we go back and look at Abraham's journey and his altar building, we see that these are two times when no reference is made to his having built an altar. There is a lesson in this for us. When are we likely to be the most vulnerable to the attacks of the evil or when are we most likely to fall before the fiery darts of the wicked? When we have failed to build an altar.

Many people have stopped building altars of worship to God.

We have left the altar of reading God's Word. We have left the altar of prayer. We have left the altar of consistently assembling with the saints.

Yes, we can trace Abraham's steps by the altars he built. And we can also find him in trouble when he was far removed from his altars. Let us take heed.

The first mention of an altar is found in Genesis 7:

1. And the LORD said unto Noah, Come thou and all thy house into the ark; for thee have I seen righteous before me in this generation.

It was the Lord (Jehovah) who invited Noah and his family into the ark, and it was the Lord who shut him in.

After the flood, it was God (Elohim) who gave the command for Noah and his family to go forth from the ark.

Genesis 8
15 And God spake unto Noah, saying,
16 Go forth of the ark, thou, and thy wife, and thy sons, and thy sons' wives with thee.

As Noah emerges into a new world, His first act is worship.

Genesis 8
20 And Noah built an altar unto the LORD; and took of every clean beast, and of every clean fowl, and offered burnt offerings on the altar.
21 And the LORD smelled a sweet savour...

It was a pleasant smell, an acceptable odor. It pleased the Lord so much that God then said...

21 (con') ...and the LORD said in his heart, I will not again curse the ground any more for man's sake; for the imagination of man's heart is evil from his youth; neither will I again smite any more everything living, as I have done.

This pleased the Lord.

We live in the New Testament era of grace, so where are our worship altars?

Why is it even important for us to ask? We no longer have need of "altars" in the Old Testament sense. But we do need altars in our lives in another way.

The altar represents true worship and involves surrender, sacrifice, and service.

Many people want to worship God in their own way, a way that involves no sacrifice whatsoever.

They want to worship as long as it is in their comfort zone. Staying in our comfort zones will not change your life, your family, your situation or your nation.

We must worship God as He requires through Jesus Christ and Him alone. He is our altar. We are to approach God in and through Him.

In Genesis 28:11-18, Jacob had a dream. He saw a ladder, angels ascending and descending and the King of Glory at the top.

When Jacob woke up, the first thing he did to commemorate the significance of finding the "door of heaven" was to build create an altar of worship.

Jacob's Altar meant 5 distinct things:

1. Encounter— Jacob had come in close contact with the creator of the universe.
2. Access— When Jacob woke from his dream, he realized that he had found the door to heaven, the place where angels were dispatched down to earth with heavenly communication, and the place where they went back up bearing human petitions. If there was any place on earth where people could interact with God, to hear and be heard, this was the spot.
3. Revelation—Jacob received clear revelation and direction about his own life. The promises of the fathers would rest upon him, and God would be with him.
4. Worship— Jacob understood that even though the dream was over, God was still there. And if God was there, that meant it was time to give something back, a token of his affection and love. He poured oil over his altar and worshipped.
5. Dwelling— Not only had Jacob encountered God, He set up a stone and named the place of His encounter, Bethel, the "house of God."

In the Old Testament, altars were made of stones. In the New Testament, something changes. The altars are made of living stones as the people of God gathered for worship and intercession.

When Jesus said He would be in the midst of His people when two or more gathered, He was changing the way people encountered God altogether.

The access that Jacob dreamed of, a single place on the earth where he met with God, has now been disseminated to the nations.

Instead of traveling to the altar, now believers can make an altar or gather and make an altar with two or three in agreement, and God sets his ladder down in the middle of their meeting. He promises to inhabit our praise so even if we are not in the midst of believers, God will come if we build an altar of worship unto Him.

We can build a dwelling place for God through continuous worship and intercession.

Look at the life of Jacob. He worked with Laban for 14 years as he waited for Rebecca,

Then Genesis 33 says:
19 And he bought a parcel of a field, where he had spread his tent...
20 And he erected there an altar and called it Elelohe-Israel.

Elelohe-Israel means the Mighty One of Israel. Jacob consecrated that place unto God.

Genesis 35 (1-7)
1 And God said unto Jacob, Arise, go up to Bethel, and dwell there: and make there an altar unto God, that appeared unto thee when thou fleddest from the face of Esau thy brother.
2 Then Jacob said unto his household, and to all that were with him, Put away the strange gods that are among you, and be clean, and change your garments:

God said 4 important things to Jacob:
1. Arise
2. Go to Bethel
3. Dwell there
4. Make an altar there

And Jacob told his household and to all who were with him to put away the foreign gods that were among them. It was time for them to purify themselves and change their garments.

3 Then let us arise and go up to Bethel; and I will make an altar there to God, who answered me in the day of my distress and has been with me in the way which I have gone.

So, they gave Jacob all the foreign gods which were in their hands, and the earrings which were in their ears; and Jacob hid them under the terebinth tree which was by Shechem.

Ultimately, God wanted his heart. And He wants the same from us.

Building this altar brought God's protection. As they journeyed, the terror of God was upon the cities that were all around them, and they did not pursue the sons of Jacob.

In Genesis 35 verse 9, we see that God spoke to Jacob again at Bethel. God appeared to Jacob when he came from Padanaram and blessed him.

Then God changed his name from Jacob to Israel.

Genesis 35

10 And God said unto him, Thy name is Jacob: thy name shall not be called any more Jacob, but Israel shall be thy name: and he called his name Israel.
11 And God said unto him, I am God Almighty: be fruitful and multiply; a nation and a company of nations shall be of thee, and kings shall come out of thy loins;
12 And the land which I gave Abraham and Isaac, to thee I will give it, and to thy seed after thee will I give the land.
13 And God went up from him in the place where he talked with him.
14 And Jacob set up a pillar in the place where he talked with him, even a pillar of stone: and he poured a drink offering thereon, and he poured oil thereon.
15 And Jacob called the name of the place where God spake with him, Bethel.

Once again, we see that Jacob set up an altar to the Lord. When Jacob finally arrived at the place God told him to go, Jacob immediately found great blessing. God appeared to him, God blessed him, and God called him by his new name, Israel,

The reminder of the new name was important because Jacob had been acting like Jacob, meaning supplanter instead of Israel, which means "he will rule as God."

God wanted him to set his mind on who He created him to be. God does the same with us, reminding us who we are in Him. God wants us to remember and live in whose image we were created.

God appeared to Jacob again and the relationship was restored. This is an excellent example of what it means to return to your first love, as in the book of Revelation.

Revelation 2
4 Nevertheless, I have somewhat against thee, because thou hast left thy first love.

Jacob remembered to go back to Bethel, he repented by getting rid of all the idols, and he did the first works by building an altar and worshipping God as before.

In the opening verse of Judges 6, it reads:
1 And the children of Israel did evil in the sight of the Lord: and the Lord delivered them into the hand of Midian seven years.

These words describe an endless cycle that repeated itself in Israel for generations. Throughout the preceding chapters, we find these words repeated again and again.

Of course, every time Israel was enslaved, they cried out to God. And each time, the Lord was faithful to send them a deliverer. But as soon as that righteous leader died, the people returned to their sin. And the whole cycle began all over again.

So, God sent a prophet who put his finger on the reason the people were being so harassed. He pointed out, "Look at your history. In each case, God delivered you out of the hands of all who oppressed you. He brought you out of bondage in Egypt. And he told you not to fear the gods of the Amorites, in whose land you dwell.

But you haven't obeyed him. You still pay homage to false gods" (see Judges 6:8-10).

The Lord was telling his people: you are not to fear anyone but me. Let no other fear enter your heart. But You've allowed fear to enter in. And you've forced me to hand you over to your enemy, to drive you back to myself."

What was this great evil that Israel kept falling back into, over and over?

They forgot the Lord's command not to fear the gods of this world. In essence, they forsook God, and also served Baalim" (Judges 10:10).

The word Baalim is a plural form. It denotes all the false gods in the world. The root of Baalim is Baal, which is a demonic spirit.

Baal's ultimate mission is to rob God of all worship and trust by his people.

It accomplishes this by focusing our attention on our circumstances rather than on the Lord. Baal means master. This spirit seeks to master you.

God is still saying to us today that He desires more from us. The Bible says that Israel wept loudly, crying out to God in their anguish. They acknowledged that they had sinned.

But there was yet another step to take to build an altar of worship. They had to tear down Baal.

The Lord spoke this word to Gideon in Judges 6:

> **25** Take thy father's young bullock, even the second bullock of seven years old, and throw down the altar of Baal that thy father hath, and cut down the grove that is by it. In other words, tear down your old methods of worship that keep you connected to old structures.

Gideon probably thought he repented sufficiently. After all, he had cried out to the Lord. He had heard the prophetic word God sent to Israel.

And he had responded to it fully, acknowledging his sin.

We see the same thing among many Christians today. We repent, cry out to God, hear the prophetic words. But there is still an idol in our midst called Baal. And before we build new worship altars, we must first tear down any altars of mistrust or unbelief.

Baal is still very much an idol today. And if our repentance is to be complete, we have to tear this idol down. Otherwise, it won't matter how much we cry out to God, pray or fast. Our actions will not have the impact we need until we pull down any idols that might be in our heart.

This is a spirit, sent forth from hell for one purpose - to cause people to doubt the reality of God. Ultimately, it is a spirit of mistrust and unbelief. it seeks to assault our minds with doubts about God's faithfulness.

Refuse to give your time to people, places or things that keep you from fully surrendering to serve God.

It is absolutely dangerous to entertain this spirit. It can infiltrate our thoughts. And once doubt and fear are allowed to enter, the Baal spirit desires to control your life. If this spirit is left unchallenged, the Baal spirit of unbelief moves in and sets up an altar.

The verse we see repeated throughout Judges - "The children of Israel did evil in the sight of the Lord" - refers not to some gross sin, but to the people's unbelief.

You will find this in Judges 2:11; Judges 3:7; Judges 3:12; Judges 4:1 and Judges 6:1.

Look around you today. There is widespread uncertainty in our society.

Bankruptcies are at an all-time high. Workers are afraid of losing their jobs.

There are earthquakes, hurricanes, volcano, terrorism, and violence like never before. As people look at the future, they're overwhelmed by fear. In times like this, Satan launches an all-out attack. He wants to get into your mind, to plant seeds and build a Baal altar. He wants you to doubt everything you've ever known about God's Word.

Now, in Judges 6, the Midianites, meaning contentious, were troubling Israel. God sent an angel to Gideon. The angel said:

Judges 6
12 The Lord is with thee, thou mighty man of valour.

He reminds Gideon that he is mighty, which is the word Gibbor. It means powerful, warrior, tyrant, champion, chief, giant, strong and valiant man.

The word Valour is the word Chayil, meaning a force, an army, wealth, virtue, valor, and strength.

God speaks the same words to us: "The Lord is with you." The Lord is saying, "My promise is all you need: I am with you."

God had already commanded Gideon, "Go, deliver Israel. I will be with you." But there was still a heart-issue to deal with.

The Lord knew that Gideon still had doubts that He was with him.

That's idolatry. It's the spirit of Baal.

God visited Gideon to reassure him that He was with him and he built an altar

> **24** Then Gideon built an altar there unto the LORD,
> and called it Jehovah shalom...

So, He instructed Gideon to get his father's bull and pull down that idol.

Then he was to cut down all the trees in the grove and use them to build a new altar. He was to consume his father's idol on that altar. God wanted him to bring down that symbol of unbelief and destroy it completely.

When Gideon pulled down the altar of Baal in his father house, the worshippers of Baal rose up against him but the Almighty God delivered him from them all.

God is about to do a new, powerful work in our lives. He is bringing us into new victories. He's about to do a new thing. But first, you must pull down every thought of doubt and lay down every fear. God wants you to tear down the spirit of Baal completely in your heart, and begin to live and speak in faith.

Put the enemy on notice: "God is with me, devil. You can't hurt me. And you can't stop His plans for my life. The Lord has victories ahead for me.

God required the same of Elijah. When Ahab and Jezebel were passionate about instituting their false religion, they erected an altar to Baal.

This shows us the devil's intentions. He wanted to establish his own altar at the place that should have been dedicated to God.

In 1 Kings 18, we see that Elijah gathered all of Israel together. God told him what was coming on the earth but the rain couldn't come until the altar was repaired. His job was to repair the altar that had been broken down.

1 Kings 18
> **21** And Elijah came unto all the people, and said, How long halt ye between two opinions? If the LORD be God, follow him: but if Baal, then follows him. And the people answered him not a word.

Halt means to do a limping dance. He was asking the people how long they would dance (go back and forth) between two opinions? The people could not even answer him!

Elijah set up the altar and challenged the prophets of Baal to call on their god. The bible says they danced before their altar all day long but no one heard them.

God instructed him to build an altar to him and call on Him. He said He would answer by fire and everyone will know that He is the Lord God.

Verse 24

24 And call ye on the name of your gods, and I will call on the name of the LORD: and the God that answereth by fire, let him be God. And all the people answered and said, It is well spoken.

There had been no rain for three and a half years. I'm sure these false prophets had cried out to their gods for intervention, but just as Baal couldn't send the fire from heaven, he was unable to send the rain as well.

When you build a new altar to God, it is then you begin to hear the sound of abundance.

After Elijah built a new altar to God, he told Ahab that he heard the sound of an abundance of rain. Say to your enemies, "I hear the sound of abundance."

Just as God was faithful to send the rain for Elijah, He will send it for you as well. If we follow Elijah's example, the heavens will open and the rain will fall.

We need to make sure the altar of the Lord is established in our lives. If it's been broken down or neglected, then it's time to repair it.

Allow Holy Spirit the opportunity to examine your hearts. Build a new altar.

When you read the story in the scripture, you will see that the fire also consumed the dust that was on the ground. The dust stands for the flesh. When you do what God asks you to do - when you build this new altar to God, the grace to overcome the things that caused us to war in our flesh and in the works of the flesh will be released.

It is not unusual to have dry seasons and rainy seasons, but as you build a new altar of worship, the coming year will be an exception because it will be a rainy season all year. Build your altar.

When this fire fell, everybody fell on their faces and said, "The Lord is God." In a single moment, God turned a whole nation to God. The altar was the priority.

But even the altar of sacrifice where you met with God today will be old tomorrow so build a new one, don't settle for the altars of yesterday. Build new ones.

It's not enough for us to tear down pagan altars and remove the priests of Baal. We must repair the Lord's altar and cry out for new fire from heaven and consumes the burnt offerings. We must be jealous for the honor of God's house and not hesitate to obey Him.

1 Kings 18
39 And when all the people saw it, they fell on their faces: and they said, The LORD, he is the God; the LORD, he is the God.

As we built new altars of worship, we will see awakening, healing, restoration, the transfer of wealth, the release of the harvest, increased revelation and nations changed. His power will be released when we worship in spirit and in truth. His Prevailing word will come forth and the angel forces will be released. Battalions of harvest angels will be released into the earth.

So, the new altar that we must build to God must be:

1. An altar of faith. We must not doubt God. Read and study Hebrews 11:

6 But without faith it is impossible to please him: for he that cometh to God must believe that he is and that he is a rewarder of them that diligently seek him. Is there anything too hard for God? Jeremiah 32:27

Build new altars of faith. Every promise of God concerning you shall be fulfilled.

Build new altars. The enemy has come to try to shake your faith but your mourning will be turned into dancing.

Build new altars. No longer will fear stop you. Boldness will be released for every new assignment in the coming year.

1. An altar of thanksgiving. It's still an altar of sacrifice.

Hebrews 13
15 By him, therefore, let us offer the sacrifice of praise to God continually, that is, the fruit of our lips giving thanks to his name.

16 And do not forget to do good and to share with others, for with such sacrifices God is pleased.

Let it be an altar of thanksgiving. Learn to thank Him. Thank Him for what He has done and thank Him because He is about to do a new thing!

Isaiah 43
18 Remember ye not the former things, neither consider the things of old.
19 Behold, I will do a new thing; now it shall spring forth; shall ye not know it? I will even make a way in the wilderness, and rivers in the desert.
21 This people have I formed for myself; they shall shew forth my praise.

Psalm 103 says:
   1 Bless the Lord oh my soul and forget not all his benefits.

Take time to write a list of all His benefits.

2. An altar of praise and worship.

Psalm 65
1 Praise waiteth for thee, O God, in Sion: and unto thee shall the vow be performed.
2 O thou that hearest prayer, unto thee shall all flesh come.

3 Iniquities prevail against me: as for our transgressions, thou shalt purge them away.
4 Blessed is the man whom thou choosest, and causest to approach unto thee, that he may dwell in thy courts: we shall be satisfied with the goodness of thy house, even of thy holy temple.

You should be able to say, God, "I trust you. Come to my house. You will find praise there."

Why would God want to come to your house if all He will get is murmuring, and complaining? If God knows that in your heart and in your home, there will be constant praise, He will draw near.

You must make up your mind that it doesn't matter what is happening, you will still build an altar to worship and praise the Lord.

Psalm 134
2 Lift up your hands in the sanctuary and praise the LORD

I Timothy 2
8 I want men everywhere to lift up holy hands in prayer, without anger or disputing.

Psalm 95
6 Come, let us bow down in worship, let us kneel before the LORD our Maker;

7 for he is our God and we are the people of his pasture, the flock under his care.

Zephaniah 3
17 The LORD thy God in the midst of thee is mighty; he will save, he will rejoice over thee with joy; he will rest in his love, he will joy over thee with singing.

PSALM 47
5 God is gone up with a shout, the LORD with the sound of a trumpet.
6 Sing praises to God, sing praises: sing praises unto our King, sing praises.
7 For God is the King of all the earth: sing ye praises with understanding.
8 God reigneth over the heathen: God sitteth upon the throne of his holiness.

PSALM 68
1 To the chief Musician, A Psalm or Song of David. Let God arise, let his enemies be scattered: let them also that hate him flee before him.
2 As smoke is driven away, so drive them away: as wax melteth before the fire, so let the wicked perish at the presence of God.

Build your altar! The presence of the Lord will come to destroy the works of the enemy.

3 But let the righteous be glad; let them rejoice before God: yea, let them exceedingly rejoice.
4 Sing unto God, sing praises to his name: extol him that rideth upon the heavens by his name JAH, and rejoice before him.

- Begin to call him names:
- Almighty God
- King of Glory
- Ancient of days
- Lion of the tribe of Judah

Build an altar of worship, a place where you can tell the Almighty God, how great He is. When you worship God, and begin to call His name,
He will rise for you.

Psalm 18
3 I will call upon the LORD, who is worthy to be praised: so, shall I be saved from mine enemies.

Amos 9:11 shows us the power of praise. God said He will restore Tabernacle of David, the place where worship was first set in order. This will cause us to possess the remnant. To possess is the word
Yaresh, meaning to occupy by driving out previous tenants, and possessing in their place. It means to seize, to rob, to disinherit, to expel, to ruin, to cast out, to consume, to destroy, to disinherit, to dispossess, to drive out and to expel,

So, our worship is so powerful that it has the power to cast out, consume, expel, destroy and dispossess the works of darkness.

We are to occupy and take possession of all that has been lost or left behind by building a tabernacle - a habitation for the presence of the Lord as we enthrone Him in our worship.

3. Build an altar of prayer. You will see His progressive destiny unfold in your life. God promises to answer prayer.

Jeremiah 33
3 Call upon me and I will answer you, and show you great and mighty things which you do not know.

He did not say He might show you, He said He will show you.

John 14
14 If ye shall ask anything in my name, I will do it.

He said if you ask anything in the name of Jesus, it will be done. Believe Him and you will get results.

5. An altar of sacrifice! You must build an altar of sacrifice. When you learn to sacrifice to God, get ready for your destiny to unfold. When God sees your sacrifice, new strength and favor will rest upon you,

Proverbs 8
34 Blessed is the man that heareth me, watching daily at my gates, waiting at the posts of my doors.
35 For whoso findeth me findeth life, and shall obtain favour of the LORD.

6. An altar of dedication and consecration.
Romans 12: 1 said you are to offer yourself as a living sacrifice.

Many of us are ready to sacrifice money; ready to give anything. As long as it does not take us out our comfort zone.

Romans 12
1 I beseech you, therefore, brethren, by the mercies of God, that ye present your bodies a living sacrifice, holy, acceptable unto God, which is your reasonable service.
2 And be not conformed to this world: but be ye transformed by the renewing of your mind, that ye may prove what is that good, and acceptable, and perfect, will of God.

Until you yourself become a living sacrifice, then that altar is not yet built.

Make yourself a living sacrifice!

Psalm 24
3 Who shall ascend into the hill of the LORD? or who shall stand in his holy place?

4 He that hath clean hands, and a pure heart; who hath not lifted up his soul unto vanity, nor sworn deceitfully.
5 He shall receive the blessing from the LORD, and righteousness from the God of his salvation.
6 This is the generation of them that seek (ask; specifically, to worship: -diligently, inquire). him, that seek thy face, O Jacob. Selah.
7 Lift up your heads, O ye gates; and be ye lift up ye everlasting doors, and the King of glory shall come in.
8 Who is this King of glory? The LORD strong and mighty, the LORD mighty in battle.
9 Lift up your heads, O ye gates; even lift them up, ye everlasting doors; and the King of glory shall come in.
10 Who is this King of glory? The LORD of hosts, he is the King of glory. Selah.

Build new altars. The mighty God will answer you by fire. He will accept you as a living sacrifice to Himself. God will build a wall of fire round about you.

Build new altars. God will send help to you, even from heaven above, He will send help to you.

Build new altars and those who are pursuing you will never be able to overtake you. It shall be well with you and God will enlarge your coast speedily.

The Heavens, as well as the Earth, are now in some dimension of conflict.

Nations are in conflict.

> *This war is over boundaries in our lives and over His prophetic destiny.*

Generations are in conflict. Families, cities, and people groups are all in conflict.

We all feel the effect of this warfare. So, we are devoted to seeing the victory of all God's people.

Warfare can create great emotional upheaval.

Warfare can produce fear. War causes our will to make choices that are not always in line with God.

This war is over boundaries in our lives and over His prophetic destiny.

In the coming days, the war over our borders and boundaries are going to shift.

We must be God's government in the earth that will use many creative forms of weapons to still the enemy and establish God's ordained boundaries.

Many things will come to distract you to try to keep you from building your worship altars. The warfare against the altar takes place in the mind.

2 Corinthians 10

4 (For the weapons of our warfare are not carnal, but mighty through God to the pulling down of strong holds;)

5 Casting down imaginations, and every high thing that exalteth itself against the knowledge of God, and bringing into captivity every thought to the obedience of Christ;

6 And having in a readiness to revenge all disobedience, when your obedience is fulfilled.

When God calls you to build an altar, you might have to make your thoughts obey God or else you will find yourself in unnecessary, low-level warfare. You rule your life by the power of Holy Spirit.

Warfare means to serve in a military campaign or to contend with carnal inclinations. You must first deal with war within yourself, then you can continually build your altar.

The children of Israel had to deal with the enemies and the giants that were in the land. It is interesting that the names of the nations they fought against could also be considered as "nations" that live within us and must be conquered.

Philistines means to wallow in self. If you are so consumed with feeling sorry for yourself, you will not be able to build the altar.

Amorites means boastful or pride. If a person has too much pride, building a worship altar for the Lord is not a necessary priority.

Hittites mean violence, fear, confusion or discouragement. Any of these areas will keep you so focused on trying to be free and you will miss the fact that freedom will come as you build the altar.

Perrizite means without walls. That means you are open to the attack of the enemy because you have not been your own gatekeeper. Freedom can be found as you build the altar.

Canaanite means to bend the knee or to humiliate. Shame is a strong enemy that keeps many people from coming to God. Do not believe the lie that He does not love you or that His throne of grace is not accessible to you.

Jebusites means to trample under foot or to be polluted. There is only one place that cleansing can take place – at the altar.

David fought the Philistines in the valley of Rephaim. Rephaim means invigorating giant. The enemy often comes to make things seem bigger than they really are.

2 Samuel 5
19 And David enquired of the LORD, saying, Shall I go up to the Philistines? wilt thou deliver them into mine hand? And the LORD said unto David, Go up: for I will doubtless deliver the Philistines into thine hand.

To go up is the word, Allah. It means to ascend in worship. God gave David the victory and showed Himself as, "*The God of the breakthrough*" as he ascended in worship in the presence of his enemies!

Build your altar. Worship from the deepest place of who you are. Worship like you knows that all you have come from God.

Until we build worship altars, we have not yet begun to dance. Until we empty ourselves of our own dances and make way for His, we have not yet begun to dance. Until the word of God becomes our daily mirror in which we look to make necessary connections and adjustments, we have not yet begun to dance.

It is not in a degree, it is not about who you know and it has nothing to do with talent. True worship has nothing to do with convenience.
Cry out for that which is real and authentic. Get lost in the presence of God.

When you receive from the presence of God, it makes you forget all else except the God who gave it all to you.

- There is no room for jealousy.
- There is no room for offense.
- Don't build an altar that crumbles when the wind blows.
- It is not based on who sees you build it.
- His presence keeps us.

When we worship passionately, void of self, He inhabits our praises. When we build worship altars, God is enthroned. He comes as judge to release His mercy or His victory against our enemies. Earth aligns with heaven. Portals open. Atmospheres shift. You live in another dimension. You see with different eyes.

Your desires change. The company you keep will change. Your focus will change. Your sphere of influence will change and you will find yourself living the most wonderful life in the center of His will….in the center of His prophetic destiny.

ACTION

Build your worship altar every day by spending as much time as possible in the presence of your King. Sing, dance, pray and listen for His voice. Learn to be still and just His presence!

7 OPENING PORTALS THROUGH WORSHIP

To walk in the anointing of God, you have to know who you are and whose you are.

Begin by listening to Holy Spirit. Hear the voice of God singing this song over you!

"The heavens are open
The heavens are open
I rejoice over you
I rejoice over you"

Now sing back to Him...
"Jesus, you are the gate
You are the door

You are the portal
You are in me and I am in you so I will sing and dance with you because you sing and dance over me."

Our Father sings and rejoices over us, let's sing and dance before Him.

In Him, we live and move and have our being. In us, He lives and moves and has His being as we manifest Him in the earth realm.

We serve a supernatural God. Everything about God is supernatural and since we are made in His image, everything about us is supernatural. Supernatural is in our DNA. Everything connected to God is supernatural.

The Bible is a supernatural book. God's word is supernatural, therefore, when we say what God says, our words are supernatural.

Everything attached to God has a supernatural manifestation.
- His love is supernatural.
- His joy is supernatural.
- His peace is supernatural.
- Our faith is supernatural.
- Our authority is supernatural.
- Praise is supernatural.
- Worship is supernatural.
- Intercession is supernatural
- The prophetic is supernatural.
- Our movements are supernatural.

Each creative expression is supernatural, including songs, dance, music, art and other creative expressions.
Let's get into supernatural thinking about the power of song and movement.

Even many African tribes, Aborigines, and other cultures used music and dance in idol worship

They know music and dance have power and authority.

Every people group have dances that are indigenous to their culture.
There is a dance to redeem each nation and people group.

The body of Christ is missing the power. They think it feels uncomfortable. Many people think to themselves, "It doesn't take all that." Sometimes our actions and words contradict what we say we believe.

We have to stop trying to bring God down to our level and begin to think like supernatural sons made in the image of Almighty God.

Let's reset our thought processes.

The human brain is programmed to understand and rationalize things.
But that is not how the supernatural realm operates.

Genesis 1

2 And the earth was without form and void, and darkness was upon the face of the deep. And the Spirit of God moved upon the face of the waters.

The Spirit of God moved (fluttered) and then He spoke. Therefore, movement preceded the sound.

Movement preceded what became tangible or visible. Holy Spirit moved, then God spoke.

Genesis 1
3 And God said, Let there be light: and there was light.

Supernaturally, light is released when Holy Spirit moves through us when we dance!

We live in a movement activated, voice-activated planet! There is no sound without movement. Even the earth is in constant movement.

The only things that don't move are dead things.

When we allow Holy Spirit to move us, it causes a stirring and an unlocking and that can cause people to see that which God wants to manifest. It brings it from the Spirit realm to the natural realm.

When movement and sound work together, light is released that literally demolishes darkness, destruction, death, ignorance, wickedness and the result is open heavens.

Movement and sound are supernatural weapons that work together.

The first recorded song in the Bible is connected to the first mention of dance. God delivered the children of Israel from many years in bondage to Pharaoh, delivered them through the Red Sea, which represents the fact that we have been delivered from death, hell and the grave and brought through the blood of Jesus!

Exodus 15
1 Then sang Moses and the children of Israel this song unto the LORD, and spake, saying, I will sing unto the LORD, for he hath triumphed gloriously: the horse and his rider hath he thrown into the sea.

So Miriam responded with a song and a dance, while she played her tambourine. It was a call and response. We see movement and song working together.

Miriam led the dance because of her relationship to the deliverer. It was significant that she was the one who led the dance because it was a custom for the closest female relative to go out to meet and greet a returning victor after they had won a battle. That's us! We are His betrothed. Jesus is our returning victory. The closer His return gets, the more you will see an increase in dancing.

Egypt was defeated, and God's people were free. When one season ends and another begins, it's time to dance and sing and enter into your new season of advancement.

Jesus has defeated our enemies! We are free! It's time to dance and sing!

As we worship, we create worship altars. Worship altars not only represent places where heaven and earth meet and the eternal realm of the Kingdom of God flows into the earth, they open portals for the atmosphere of Heaven to impact the atmosphere of earth.

Who is worshipped at the altars of a territory sets the atmosphere? Worship is not just about intimacy. Worship has to do with who wins the war in the territory for a people group or a nation, for individuals, families, and communities.

There was a gathering of worshipers at a conference in Chicago. I was scheduled to speak. God woke me up and said, "Just release

My names into the atmosphere through song, dance, sound worship and praise."

When we gathered, I shared what I had heard from Holy Spirit.

We worshipped, danced, released the sounds of God and the names of God and set the atmosphere in the city. A political rally had been scheduled. These rallies were known to result in violence. As we released the names of God into the atmosphere, we won the war and the spirit of violence could not manifest. The rally was canceled! Glory to God!

Worship gives us supernatural power to rule in the midst of our enemies! We were born to rule. It's our inheritance, our birthright.

God's original intent was for Him to rule in heaven and for us to rule in the earth.

How do we rule through worship?

Psalm 110
1 A Psalm of David. The LORD said unto my Lord, Sit at my right hand...until I make thine enemies thy footstool.

To sit at the right hand of an earthly king was a place of honor, a place of special trust and authority because of the relationship with the king.

If you were to sit at the right hand of a king, it meant that you could act with his authority. Those who came to you would treat you with the same respect as they would treat the king.

The word Sit means to sit in ambush. It implies a surprise attack by people lying in wait in a concealed position.

Praise, worship, song, and dance is the supernatural, surprise ambush that opens portals to victory and triumph!

The enemy wants you to sit around, cry and have a pity party. But God says. "I have already given you what you need to win every battle."

2 The LORD shall send the rod of thy strength out of Zion: rule thou in the midst of thine enemies.

The word rod is the Hebrew word Mattah, which means a ruling scepter.

To rule means to tread down, to subjugate, to crumble, to have dominion, to prevail against and to reign.

Where are we to rule? "In the midst of thine enemies." Hallelujah! Our enemies will see the triumph given to us by our God!

3 Thy people shall be willing in the day of thy power,

Power is the word chayil, meaning force, strength, wealth army, might and power. The root word of Chayil is Chuwl, meaning to dance.

This is the day when God's power will be seen in the dance!

This is the day when His supernatural power dances will release strength, wealth, power and complete victory!

Do you remember reading in the book of Daniel about the three Hebrew boys, Shadrach, Meshach and Abednego who fell down bound in the fire?

Daniel 3
> **24** Then Nebuchadnezzar the king was astonied and rose up in haste, and spake, and said unto his counselors, Did not we cast three men bound into the midst of the fire? They answered and said unto the king, True, O king. **25** He answered and said, Lo, I see four men loose, walking in the midst of the fire, and they have no hurt; and the form of the fourth is like the Son of God.

Walking is the Hebrew word Halak, meaning to whirl. God danced in the fire with them! They ruled in the midst of their enemies.

What kind of men were they, that could dance in the midst of the fire and not get burned? Supernatural!

We know that David danced! He was a chayil man. He found out that sometimes the enemy you are ordained to rule over is in your own house.

2 Samuel 6
> **16** And as the ark of the LORD came into the city of David, Michal Saul's daughter looked through a window, and saw

king David leaping and dancing before the LORD; and she despised him in her heart.

21 And David said unto Michal, It was before the LORD, which chose me before thy father, and before all his house, to appoint me ruler over the people of the LORD, over Israel: therefore will I play before the LORD. **22** And I will yet be more vile than thus, and will be based in mine own sight: and of the maidservants which thou hast spoken of, of them shall I be had in honor. **23** Therefore Michal the daughter of Saul had no child unto the day of her death.

So, David ruled over all of Israel and he ruled in the midst of his enemies. Dance exposes religious spirits and keeps that spirit from reproducing. It becomes barren.

David understood something about worship and how to keep portals of victory open through praise.

That is why David said:

Psalm 34

1 I will bless the LORD at all times: his praise shall continually be in my mouth.

To bless is the word Barak, which means to kneel. Our movement (kneeling) and our voice (praise) activate deliverance.

2 My soul shall make her boast in the LORD: the humble shall hear thereof, and be glad.

Boast means Halal, and it suggests movement, sound, and color.

3 O magnify the LORD with me, and let us exalt his name together.

4 I sought the LORD, and he heard me and delivered me from all my fears.

Open your mouth and praise the Lord! You have to say something to open the heavens to receive revelation and manifestation of deliverance from all your fears.

7 The angel of the LORD encampeth round about them that fear him and delivereth them.

The angels are released!

8 O taste and see that the LORD is good: blessed is the man that trusteth in him.

Your senses are activated to taste and see.

The Authority of the Feet

Take a few seconds to look at your feet. Feet represent authority. Joshua 1:3 tells us that every piece of ground the soles of our feet tread upon, God has given to us. Everything belongs to our Father; therefore, it belongs to us.

Psalm 18

29 For by thee I have run through a troop, and by my God have I leaped over a wall.

We are not to be afraid! We are to rush on the enemy speedily and jump over them.

32 It is God that girdeth me with strength, and makes my way perfect.

He gives us Chayil strength to dance. His dance maketh my way perfect.

There is a supernatural dance of strength that will open portals and set the course for your future

33 He maketh my feet like hinds' feet and sets me upon my high places.

To have hinds 'feet means you have agility, swiftness, sure-footedness that makes you able to escape or outrun your enemies.

Ancient warriors fought on foot. They had to be swift to run from place to place, give orders, attack their enemies and defend their friends.
The high places were places of safety or refuge. High places represent security and safety from danger.

34 He teaches my hands to war...

36 Thou hast enlarged my steps under me, that my feet did not slip.

37 I have pursued mine enemies, and overtaken them: neither did I turn again till they were consumed.

38 I have wounded them that they were not able to rise: they are fallen under my feet.

39 For thou hast girded me with (chayil) strength unto the battle: thou hast subdued under me those that rose up against me.

40 Thou hast also given me the necks of mine enemies; that I might destroy them that hate me.

When you run, it is a supernatural running through spiritual obstacles that try to hold you in a tight place.

Portals of victory are opened by the power in your feet.

Darkness will flee, sickness will crumble by your move! Run, kick, spin and give a victorious clap and a thunderous shout!

Look at Malachi 4:2b-3. This is how to defeat the enemy

2 and ye shall go forth, and grow up as calves of the stall

3 And ye shall tread down the wicked; for they shall be ashes under the soles of your feet in the day that I shall do this, saith the LORD of hosts.

When you get in a tight place, start singing and dancing. God has supernatural songs of deliverance. He also has supernatural dances of deliverance.

Someone will ask you, "How did you get out of that situation?" You will reply, "God gave me a song and a dance."

There are songs of victory and dances of victory.

There are songs of healing and dances of healing.

I remember a time when I had excruciating pain behind my eyes. I remember the pain going away as we began to worship.

On another occasion, our dance group was ministering in dance at a church in Atlanta. It was a simple dance representing the holiness of God. We danced with small votive candles. As we began to walk up the aisle with the candles, we heard a woman scream, only to find out that God had healed her during the worship. Hallelujah!

There are also songs of war and dances of war. When we marry the war song with the war movement and come forth as God's dancing calves, watch God turn the tables on the enemy.

Our feet represent authority and the wicked become like dust under our feet. When we release the dance that lies dormant in our spirits it releases His triumph. You must not remain silent in your praise. It's supernatural.

You may not be physically able to leap and dance around, but you must not be passive in worship. When you hold back your praises, the portal can't open that allows us to sow to the heavens so the glory can be released in the earth realm.

God will supernaturally accelerate the manifestation of your victory!

Just enter in to praise. Supernatural means intervention of divine laws. Since we are made in the image of God, we are not subject to the same laws as the rest of the natural world.

Imagine what would have happened if Paul and Silas had been silent.

They worshipped, and sang praises and celebrated God so loud (Acts 16) that not only did all the prisoners hear them, the earth itself reacted in such a way that the foundations of the prison were shaken. And immediately all the doors were opened, and everyone's bands were loosed. The supernatural portal of freedom and deliverance was opened.

Paul and Silas were not quiet, they were not still. They didn't have time to be in prison! They didn't have time to wait for a trial!

Praise supernaturally accelerated their freedom by opening a portal that created an unstoppable momentum. You can find yourself caught up in a move of God that will shift your circumstances, remove obstacles and command a manifestation of freedom beyond that which the natural mind can comprehend.

Remember Jehoshaphat? We read in 2 Chronicles 20 how the enemy came against the people of God but they sought the Lord.

2 Chronicles 20
> **18** And Jehoshaphat bowed his head with his face to the ground: and all Judah and the inhabitants of Jerusalem fell before the LORD, worshipping the LORD.

Sometimes all you need to do is bow and put your face to the ground!

2 Chronicles 20
> 21 And when he had with the people, he appointed singers unto the LORD, and that should praise the beauty of holiness, as they went out before the army, and to say, Praise the LORD; for his mercy endureth forever.
> 22 And when they began to sing and to praise, the LORD set ambushments against the children of Ammon, Moab, and mount Seir, which werec ome against Judah; and they were smitten.

Notice that the LORD set ambushments against the enemy. Israel didn't kill them, the Lord Himself defeated them. Praise caused the heavens to open and there were a victory and a supernatural acceleration of provision.

The power for supernatural acceleration is in the eternal realm of worship and it will cause the plowman to overtake the reaper in your health, family, finances and in every area of your life.

Seeds of worship that have been sown in the past are full-grown and ready for reaping.

And When the realm of Glory moves into the realm of the natural, there comes an acceleration for creative miracles, healing, signs, and wonders.

Supernatural songs, sounds, and dances of power and authority can result in breakthrough in cities, states, and nations.

Let us learn to hear the drumbeat of the Lord...hear the sound He is releasing and the dance He is ordaining, discerning His times and seasons, and cooperating with Him to fulfill His plans on the earth.

We have these two supernatural weapons...sound and movement.

> *He's calling for this army of divine destroyers to shout, sing and dance in his portal and destroy the enemy.*

Exodus 15

3 The LORD *is* a man of war: The LORD is his name.

Jeremiah 50

25 The LORD hath opened his armory, (treasury) and hath brought forth the weapons (vessels) of his indignation: for this is the work of the Lord GOD of hosts.

We are his treasury, we are his vessels and our dance is part of His spiritual arsenal. He is Lord Sabaoth, the Lord of a mass of people organized for war.

Isaiah 13

4 There's a loud noise on the mountain that sounds like a large army. The Lord who commands armies is gathering His forces for battle.

He's calling for this army of divine destroyers to shout, sing and dance in his portal and destroy the enemy.

When necessary, there must be a militancy in our movements. Dances were often done in a row or in a ring. They were done in rank like a company or an army of dancers. We are His army and we must take our place in the ranks. That includes all of us.

Warfare is strategy. We must know our weapons. We must know what song to sing, what dance to dance. We don't bring forth the same sound or the same dance in every situation.

We bring forth a different song and dance against the stronghold of the lingering effects of apartheid in South Africa than in red light district of Holland, or in a country like Iraq that has been torn by violence.

Since death and life are in power of the tongue, use your sound to manifest victory.

God inhabits our praises, He comes to sit as judge. His full authority comes. Then, in the midst of our worship, He executes His judgment against our enemies.

Where the spirit of the Lord is there is liberty! Freedom! So, stand up right where you are, begin to march in place, clap your hands and shout. Marching always speaks of advancement. You might say,

"That's just not me." You are right! It's the Spirit of God who wants to testify of Jesus through you. You might say, 'I can't sing or dance." I have good news for you! Holy Spirit can! So, let Him sing and move through you.

The Psalms are songs. Be free to sing and dance in the presence of the Lord. Sing a new song, dance a new dance.

Psalm 149

1 Praise ye the LORD. Sing unto the LORD a new song, and his praise in the congregation of saints.
2 Let Israel rejoice (jump for joy) in him that made him: let the children of Zion be joyful in their King.
3 Let them praise his name in the dance: let them sing praises unto him with the timbrel and harp.
4 For the LORD taketh pleasure in his people: he will beautify the meek with salvation.
5 Let the saints be joyful in glory: let them sing aloud upon their beds.
6 Let the high praises (exalted shouts of God be in their mouth, and a two-edged sword in their hand;
7 To execute vengeance upon the heathen, and punishments upon the people;
8 To bind their kings with chains, and their nobles with fetters of iron;
9 To execute upon them the judgment written: this honour have all his saints. Praise ye the LORD.

Our weapons are not carnal, but they are mighty, and they are powerful to cause damage with both the back of the sword and the edge of the sword. We strike with our sword, and we strike with our shout. Whichever way we move, we strike deadly blows at the enemy.

Sing and dance your way into a new dimension of worship! Break free from the constraints of the natural realm. Shake off old paradigms that would keep you in a place of bondage. Begin to live in the supernatural realm of worship so you can rule in the midst of your enemies.

Psalm 67
5 Let the people praise thee, O God; let ALL the people praise thee. (Let them yadah, meaning to out the hands in worship and give thanks)
6 Then shall the earth yield her increase; and God, even our own God, shall bless us.

ACTION

Here are 5 songs that the Lord gave to me. Feel free to dance and sing them to the melody God gives you!

SONG OF VICTORY
We lift up our shout to our King
We establish the gates of praise
We possess the gates of the enemy
The gates of hell will not prevail

I stake my claim for my territory
I crush the head of my adversaries
We possess the gates of the enemy
The gates of hell will not prevail

SONG FOR ISRAEL
Hear oh Israel, Hear His Chariots
Take Your Shield, release a Battle Cry
Behold Your Messiah is here to save
Yes! Your King is mighty to save

SONG OF ARROWS
The arrow of the Lord of Hosts is released
Shoot Your Arrows, destroy all our enemies
Mighty king, awesome deliverer
All our enemies will fall at our feet

SONG OF JUSTICE
Let justice come
Let justice prevail
The voice of Holy Spirit be heard
Let justice come

Let justice prevail
Let Your glory cover the earth

SONG FOR THE KING
We worship with our dances of war
We worship with our shouts of war
Shoot your arrows of glory
Make me a sword in your hand

To break the chains of the enemy
As we dance in the portals of our God
Sound aloud your war horn
Shout out King in our midst

8 EVANGELIZING THE NATION

Let me take just a few minutes to share my story. I came to know Christ when I was dancing in a Broadway show called 42nd Street. Once I became a Christian, our church took a ministry outreach trip to Hawaii. I would sit on the balcony of the hotel each morning and worship. One morning, God spoke to me and told me that He would take me all over the world to dance for Him. I didn't do anything to try to fulfill His prophetic words for my life. I just spent time in His presence each day, worshipped, prayed and studied His word. Doors of ministry began to open and I have seen Him fulfill His purposes for my life. All praise be to God!

The Bible tells us that God loves the world. That means that God wants us to have a global vision because it is His vision. As it says in the book of Revelation:

Revelation 5
> **9** And they sung a new song, saying, Thou art worthy to take the book, and to open the seals thereof: for thou wast slain, and hast redeemed us to God by thy blood out of every kindred, and tongue, and people, and nation;
> **10** And hast made us unto our God kings and priests: and we shall reign on the earth.

There is an end-time harvest we must bring in. We must know our prophetic destiny so we can help bring others into the kingdom.

Matthew 9:35-38
> **35** And Jesus went about all the cities and villages, teaching in their synagogues, and preaching the gospel of the kingdom, and healing every sickness and every disease among the people.
> **36** But when he saw the multitudes, he was moved with compassion on them, because they fainted, and were scattered abroad, as sheep having no shepherd.
> **37** Then saith he unto his disciples, The harvest truly is plenteous, but the labourers are few;
> **38** Pray ye, therefore, the Lord of the harvest, that he will send forth labourers into his harvest.

Luke 19:10 tells us that Jesus came to seek and save the lost. Ask for God's heart for the nations and for those who do not know our King.

We must understand the enormity of the mandate of the Ekklesia in these last days. It is harvest time.

Are you willing to be a laborer?

Are you willing to go across town or across the world? Will you carry the living water to those who are thirsty?

God's desire is to have a functioning, alive, indigenous, reproducing church in every nation and among every people group.

As God sends us to bring in the harvest, we must remember that there are two parts to effectively reaching the lost:

1. The actual message
2. The delivery system that gets the message to the desired target - the hearts of the people

1. The actual message

Remember - it is God's message, not yours. In John 4:34, Jesus said he came to "do the will of Him who sent me."

This is especially true when dealing with other people groups in other countries. More than likely, they have a different culture than the culture you are used to. That means they might have different thoughts, different mindsets. You cannot judge them because of their culture. Culture is what defines a people group. It represents what they have in common. Ask for a global perspective and for the heart of God for every people group.

I have been to nations where it is cultural to use the hips in dance, other nations where men dance with bare chests and yet another nation where breastfeeding in public is the norm. None of those cultural behaviors would be easily accepted in the part of the United States that I grew up in.

There are even some words that do not translate well. When we were in Fiji, we learned that the word Bula means hello! So, we bought shirts that say, Bula! We then traveled to St. Lucia and decided to wear our Bula shirts. A gentleman in St. Lucia quickly informed us that Bula does not mean hello in St. Luca. In fact, in St. Lucia, Bula means you are a homosexual. Since we are not homosexuals, it was not our intent to communicate that so we quickly took the shirts off.

When I visited Australia, they asked if I wanted someone to billet me. Since I didn't know the meaning of the word, I was not sure if I wanted someone to billet me. I found out that it means to stay in someone's home. Someone did billet me. Once I arrived, I was told that my luggage would be put in the boot. In the boot? The boot is the trunk of the car.

I attended an international dance and worship gathering in Scotland. While there, I encountered a worshipping belly dancer. I had never seen that before in the church so I enquired about her culture, only to be told that belly dancing was accepted in the nation in which she lived.

Rev 7:9 tells us that "every tribe and tongue" will worship. Heaven celebrates cultures. He made us different.

I was so blessed by dance ministers I saw from Singapore. They had redeemed one of their cultural dances. The dance is done by hitting two long poles together in a rhythm on the floor. The "redeemed version" represents not being ensnared or trapped by the enemy. Another culture dance is done gracefully with lighted candles in votives held on top of the head. The "redeemed dance" represented the day of Pentecost in Acts 2:

3 And there appeared unto them cloven tongues like as of fire, and it sat upon each of them.

There are nations that are steeped in poverty. In other nations, alcohol ravages many people. Gang violence is a daily norm. Drug lords rule.
Promiscuity can be seen easily. But God has a plan.

In order to discover the prophetic destiny of your nation, study all you can about your nation, including understanding the cultural differences and dimensions. We cannot expect to minister the same way in every country.

Cultural differences include:
- Money we must know the exchange rate and the financial history of the nation.
- Government
- Customs
- Dress
- Climate
- Food
- Language
- Thought processes

Some nations are steeped in strict religious structures that have been in place for years. Other countries have no religious freedom at all. In Muslim countries, it would not be wise to try to force

Christianity on anyone. We must pray and ask the Lord for His wisdom. We cannot beat people over the head with a bible!

God has different ways, different methods and different strategies of reaching every heart. Ask God for His wisdom, His method, and His strategy. Jesus did. He did not always minister the same way with those He came in contact with.

Worship arts (dance, music, painting) is a great tool for evangelism. People remember more of what they see than what they hear.

My husband and I have had the privilege of ministering at a wonderful worship arts conference in Germiston, South Africa near Johannesburg. They are one of the most effective ministries in using the arts – mime, drama, music, song, painting, art, dance and even puppets. They have been very successful in taking the arts into secular theaters to evangelize the lost. They know what appeals to their culture. What tools would be effective in your nation?

Once you discover that, go even beyond the method. Go to the message.

Ask God what He wants to say. Then ask how He wants to say it. Then be open and walk in obedience to His instructions, even if you don't understand them.

Once He touched someone and they were healed.

Matthew 8:

> 14 And when Jesus was come into Peter's house, he saw his wife's mother laid, and sick of a fever.
> 15 And he touched her hand, and the fever left her: and she arose, and ministered unto them.
> 16 says He casts out spirits with His word. He spoke and people were delivered.

16 When the even was come, they brought unto him many that were possessed with devils: and he cast out the spirits WITH HIS WORD, and healed all that were sick:

Another time, Jesus spat on the ground. John 9:6 says,

6 When he had thus spoken, he spat on the ground and made clay of the spittle, and he anointed the eyes of the blind man with the clay,

7 And said unto him, Go, wash in the pool of Siloam, (which is by interpretation, Sent.) He went his way, therefore, and washed, and came seeing.

No matter what strategy we use, we must hear from the Lord and walk in obedience as we minister biblically and with boldness.

Have you shared your faith with others? Do you feel comfortable sharing your faith? We must communicate the Gospel clearly. Be willing to be God messengers.

Let us empty ourselves of our own dances, our own songs, our own ways and methods of operating so we can make way for His.

Ask God these questions:
- Are you sending me to gather for worship?
- Are you sending me into war?
- Are you sending me in to cry out for repentance?
- Are you sending me in to comfort your people?

Perhaps you will be sent for all of these purposes at one time or another.

We cannot worry about being rejected, embarrassed or humiliated. It is His message. We have only to obey Him.

When I visited the Netherlands several years ago, I found it to be a rather promiscuous culture. When I went to buy a souvenir to take home, I found sexually centered magazines out in the open right next to the souvenirs I was trying to purchase! Culture!

I have stayed in countries where the lights would go out at any moment and hot water for a shower was not expected. Culture!

Once when visiting another country, a reservation was made for me in a hotel where the room had no toilet in the room! The bathroom was down the hall. Culture!

Once on a trip to Israel, we actually stayed in a hotel that was located in the Arab quarters. They were warm (and curious) and very accommodating to our "culture" of worship.

World evangelism statistics stand as follows: Of the 55 least evangelized countries, 97% of their population still lives within what is called the 10/40 Window.

Unless something changes soon, is it possible that huge numbers of these unreached people will never hear the Gospel? Studies show that it is estimated that only about 10% of the global missionary force is working in these areas because open evangelism is difficult and sometimes impossible because of governmental restrictions in many 10/40 Window countries.

Here are mission statistics and facts to consider from the places of the 10/40 Window:

- The 10/40 window is the center of population: Two-thirds of the world's population -- more than 4.4 billion people -- live in the 10/40 Window.

- 90% of the people living in the 10/40 Window are unreached and un-evangelized. Many have never heard the Gospel message at all.

- There are either no Christians or not enough of a Christian movement in many cultures of the 10/40 Window to carry out evangelism.

If those groups are to be evangelized, believers will need to leave their own culture and be willing to enter a different culture where they will seek to plant the gospel, perhaps even learning a new language in order to communicate.

This cross-cultural evangelism is required because there are people groups with no church movements that are relevant enough to bring change to them.

The good news is there is a difference between unreached and unreachable. In 1989 there were only four known Christians living in Mongolia. That country now has an estimated 10,000 indigenous believers. Also, Christian television programming can now be received in many 10/40 Window nations that were once closed.

- Eighty-five percent of those living in the 10/40 window are the poorest of the world's poor.

The good news is that Christians often deliver more than $1 million worth of food to just one 10/40 Window refugee camp in one calendar year. In one North African country that is hostile to the Gospel, abundant rain fell after a Resurrection Day service. A local news channel reported, "Christians have brought rain to the desert."

Of the known world religions, Islam, Buddhism, and Hinduism are centered within the 10/40 Window.

Here are some staggering statistical data on unreached people groups.

- There are 865 million unreached Muslims or Islamic followers in 3330 cultural sub-groupings
- 550 million unreached Hindus in 1660 cultural sub-groups
- 150 million unreached Chinese in 830 groups
- 275 million unreached Buddhists in 900 groups
- 2550 unreached tribal groups with a total population of 140 million

Forming a smaller, though important, unreached group are the 17 million Jews scattered across 134 countries.

Research shows that the country with the most rapid Christian expansion ever is China where there are 10,000 new Christian converts every day.

At least some part of Scripture has been translated into 2,212 of the world's 6,500 languages. 366 languages have the entire Bible. 928 other languages have the New Testament.

Individual books (such as the Gospel of John) are available in 918 additional languages. 80 percent of the world's people have access to at least some portion of the Bible in a language they can understand.

Below is a list of countries in the area designated as the 10/40 Window. Let's shout for the walls to come down!

Afghanistan	India	Oman
Algeria	Iran	Pakistan
Bahrain	Iraq	Philippines
Bangladesh	Israel	Portugal
Benin	Japan	Qatar
Bhutan	Jordan	Saudi Arabia
Burkina Faso	Korea, North	Senegal
Cambodia	Korea, South	Sudan
Chad	Kuwait	Syria
China	Laos	Taiwan
Cyprus	Lebanon	Tajikistan
Djibouti	Libya	Thailand
Egypt	Macau	Tunisia
Eritrea	Mali	Turkey
Ethiopia	Malta	Turkmenistan
Gambia	Mauritania	United Arab Emirates
Gibraltar	Morocco	Vietnam
Greece	Myanmar (Burma)	Western Sahara
Guinea	Nepal	Yemen
Guinea-Bissau	Niger	

Some mission strategists have divided the world's population into three groupings: World A, World B, and World C.

World A is made up of those areas where the population is considered to be less than half evangelized.

World B are those areas where the population is over 50% evangelized.

World C are those areas of the world that are at least 60% evangelized, even if only nominally.

As believers in Christ, what can we do in order to tear down walls and bring people into the kingdom?

We must be healed first in order to bring healing. Only free people can free people. Only healed people can heal people. Many Christians have an identity crisis. They don't know the power of God that lives in them.

In 1 Peter 2 chapter 2, verse 9, we are told that we are a "chosen generation, a royal priesthood, a holy nation." Let's stop acting, looking and dressing like beggars! Let's act and live like the kings we were created to be. We must show the world who our God is! All that was in Christ is in us. All means all! We are to take the good news of salvation to them. We are to introduce them to the God kind of life that includes health, prosperity, joy, peace, love, and success in every area of life!

John 10:10 says that Jesus came to give abundant life to all who believe in Him. Abundant life means abundant in quantity and superior in quality.

The world is waiting for us! Romans 8:

18 For I reckon that the sufferings of this present time are not worthy to be compared with the glory which shall be revealed in us.

19 For the earnest expectation of the creature waiteth for the manifestation of the sons of God.

As believers in Christ, what can we do? We can pray, fast, give and go!

Arise and shine for Jesus in the Nations. Let us rise up as gatekeepers and rebuild the walls that have been burned down, even as Nehemiah did. Let us take the good news of the Gospel of Jesus Christ to every nation so we can see the heart of God fulfilled and His prophetic destiny made visible.

Be willing to be a sent one! Every day you are sent into the sphere of authority God has assigned you.

For some, it is your neighborhood, your family, your friends, your job, your city, your state, your nation...and for others, their sphere encompasses nations

So, are you willing for God to send you? This is another way that we can identify with Christ and fulfill our prophetic destiny.

God is a sending God. Tradition keeps people sitting Sunday after Sunday, and it keeps them in a place of focusing only on themselves. Many who are called to be world changers are unhappy pew sitters. But God didn't call you to just to sit.

He called you so He could train you, equip you and send you.

God is a sending God. Let's look at a few scriptures that verify this truth.

Genesis 24 reads as follows:
> **7** The LORD God of heaven, …. spake unto me, saying, Unto thy seed will I give this land; he shall SEND his angel before thee…

Exodus 3
> **10** And God said to Moses, I will SEND you to Pharaoh…

> **14** And He said, "Thus you shall say to the children of Israel, 'I AM has SENT me to you."

Malachi 4
> **5** Behold, I will SEND you Elijah the prophet before the coming of the great and dreadful day of the Lord.

John 1
> 6 There was a man SENT from God, whose name was John.

John 3
> **17** For God did not SEND His Son into the world to condemn the world, but that the world through Him might be saved.

1 John 4
> **14** And we have seen and testify that the Father has SENT the Son as Savior of the world.

Acts 3
> **26** To you first, God, having raised up His Servant Jesus, SENT Him to bless you, in turning away every one of you from your iniquities.

Matthew 10
> **5** These twelve Jesus SENT out and commanded them…

Matthew 10

16 Behold, I SEND you out as sheep in the midst of wolves.

Luke 10

1 After these things, the Lord appointed seventy others also and SENT them two by two before His face into every city and place where He Himself was about to go.

John 20

21 So Jesus said to them again, "Peace to you! As the Father has SENT Me, I also SEND you."

John 14

26 But the Helper, the Holy Spirit, whom the Father will SEND in My name, He will teach you all things, and bring to your remembrance all things that I said to you.

Galatians 4

6 And because you are sons, God has SENT forth the Spirit of His Son into your hearts, crying out, "Abba, Father!"

Acts 13

4 So, being SENT out by the Holy Spirit, they went down to Seleucia, and from there they sailed to Cyprus.

Acts 8

14 Now when the apostles who were at Jerusalem heard that Samaria had received the word of God, they SENT Peter and John to them.

Acts 11
> **22** Then news of these things came to the ears of the church in Jerusalem, and they SENT out Barnabas to go as far as Antioch.

Philippians 2
> **19** But I trust in the Lord Jesus to SEND Timothy to you shortly, that I also may be encouraged when I know your state.

Philippians 2
> **25** Yet I considered it necessary to SEND to you Epaphroditus, my brother, fellow worker, and fellow soldier, but your messenger and the one who ministered to my need.

1 Thessalonians 3
> **2** And [I] SENT Timothy, our brother, and minister of God, and our fellow laborer in the gospel of Christ, to establish you and encourage you concerning your faith.

In Acts 19, we read a very interesting story.

They were some vagabond Jews who were attempting to cast out demons.

> **15** And the evil spirit answered and said, "Jesus I know, and Paul I know, but who are you?"

The spirit realm recognizes the power and authority of sent ones so the demons recognized both Jesus and Paul. Sent ones have the ability to impact the spirit realm.

On the other hand, demons don't recognize those who just went without being SENT.

Matthew 9
> **38** Therefore pray the Lord of the harvest to send out laborers into His harvest.

Luke 10
> **2** Then He said to them, "The harvest truly is great, but the laborers are few; therefore, pray the Lord of the harvest to send out laborers into His harvest."

The sending anointing is an apostolic anointing that is available to every believer.

We should be in a church where we can understand how to evangelize the lost, be trained for the work of the ministry and be sent to bring change and advance the kingdom of God.

What are we to do as we go? The word apostle was a word used by Alexander the Great describing the individuals who were responsible for acclimating a nation to the customs and protocols of Alexander's Kingdom.

Whenever Alexander conquered a territory, apostolic teams were sent out to establish his jurisdiction within the nation that had been conquered in war.

The sending of an apostle by a King meant that one Kingdom had been overthrown and another was now taking over.

This means that 500 years before Jesus was born, the word apostle had already gained cultural significance and relevance.

Matthew 10:2 lists the names of the apostles of Jesus. Many just know them as the disciples but they were apostles. So, the apostles of Jesus were introduced to the world 3 years before the church was even established.

Matthew 10

5 These twelve Jesus sent forth,
and commanded them, saying, Go not into the way of
the Gentiles, and into any city of the Samaritans enter ye not:
6 But go rather to the lost sheep of the house of Israel.
7 And as ye go, preach, saying, The kingdom of heaven is at hand.
8 Heal the sick, cleanse the lepers, raise the dead,
cast out devils: freely ye have received, freely give.
9 Provide neither gold, nor silver, nor brass in your purses,
10 Nor scrip for your journey, neither two coats, neither shoes
nor yet staves: for the workman is worthy of his meat.
11 And into whatsoever city or town ye
shall enter, inquire who in it is worthy; and there abide till ye
go thence.
12 And when ye come into a house, salute it.
13 And if the house be worthy,
let your peace come upon it: but if it be not worthy,
let your peace return to you.
14 And whosoever shall not receive you, nor hear your words,
when ye depart out of that house or city,
shake off the dust of your feet.
15 Verily I say unto you, It shall be more tolerable for
the land of Sodom and Gomorrha in the day of judgment, than for
that city.

***16** Behold, I send you forth as sheep in the midst of wolves: be ye, therefore, wise as serpents, and harmless as doves.*

He sent them out as apostles with a diplomatic anointing. The people also knew that an apostle did not show up unless the kingdom that they represented had already come to take over the territory.

Therefore, when Jesus sent the apostles He didn't instruct them to preach that the Kingdom was coming but that the Kingdom of God was already at hand.

So, the Apostles were commanded by the Lord and sent to be a light to the nations.

We all have an end-times commission to the nations.

Apostle John Eckhardt said:
"The Lord is raising up a new breed of believers with an end-times apostolic and prophetic anointing to shake nations and establish strong local churches.

The power of the Holy Spirit is given to us to touch nations. We need to prepare believers with a vision for the world.

The Lord is now raising up international churches and ministries with an apostolic anointing to train and release people in the fullness of the Holy Spirit's power.

The Lord is raising up spiritual diplomats to execute an end-time foreign policy.

He is releasing divine strategies to the Church for the end times.

These diplomats are receiving their commission from heaven and are going forth with full authority and power as ambassadors of Christ."

2 Corinthians 5
20 Now then we are ambassadors for Christ...

An ambassador is a diplomatic official of the highest rank, sent by a sovereign or state to another as its resident representative. They are the senior members of His counsel.

Notice the definition for ambassador includes the highest rank. Because of this rank, ambassadors have the authority to speak on behalf of the government that sent them.

We are ambassadors and diplomats raised up and sent by the Lord, not people sent by man.

The Lord is raising up ambassador churches and ministries that will impact the nations of the earth and help you stay in the momentum and the timing of God.

And God wants to send us to the lost and the broken. The world needs His light and He wants us to release His sent ones to bring in the end time harvest.

Every generation needs people who are willing to lay down their lives for the sake of the Gospel.

We are called to invade new nations and territories. Many people in the world are in need of a breakthrough!

The word "breakthrough" is defined as an act or instance of breaking through an obstruction; an offensive thrust that penetrates and carries beyond a defensive line in warfare.

Sent ones with a breakthrough anointing have the ability to break through ignorance, fear and other obstacles that keep people from advancing.

Someone must have the courage, ability, and power to break through the obstacles set up by the enemy that keeps people in darkness.

We must be able to discern the strongholds in each nation in order to break through tradition, religion, ignorance, poverty, witchcraft, pride, rebellion and other obstacles.

Nations, cities, and regions will open up to the Gospel because of this breakthrough anointing.

Without this anointing, these areas will remain closed to the truth.
This is why it is so difficult to break through in some cities, nations or groups of people. These areas and people need sent ones.

Will you let God send you?

The result will be that the people who need to enter the kingdom will hear the Word of God—and the church will be that much closer to fulfilling its mission.

ACTION

Ask God which nations He would have you dance over. Study as much as you can about the nation (s). There is no distance in the spirit. Get a map or a globe and begin to dance and sing!

9 GATEKEEPERS

The Bible speaks much about gates. Just as there are gatekeepers in the natural realm, God has called us to be gatekeepers in the spiritual realm.

When you fly on an airplane, you cannot board the plane unless you have a ticket. The ticket agents act as gatekeepers. Their job is to keep anyone off the plane who may cause any harm. You cannot check into a hotel unless you first stop by the gatekeeper at the front desk to secure a room.

The gatekeepers were very important. In 1 Chronicles 9:17-27, the gatekeepers were mentioned with the singers and musicians.

They were appointed and chosen by the King and they had daily responsibilities in the temple. They had to be loyal and trustworthy. They were responsible for the safety of the temple.

There were keepers of the temple gates and keepers of the city gates. They were able to refuse or admit entrance to anyone. Gatekeepers were put in place for the protection of the temple or the city.

The Bible mentions gates quite a bit. Matthew 7

13-14" ...wide is the gate, and broad is the way, that leads to destruction... straight is the gate, and narrow is the way, which leads to life..."

In Matthew 16:18, Jesus tells us that the "gates of hell shall not prevail" against the church.

Psalm 100

4 Enter into His gates with thanksgiving, and into His courts with praise..."

So, we see that heaven has gates and hell has gates.

Gates and walls were built for the protection of the city. When one was said to possess the gate of his enemy, it meant that the person had gained a position of wealth and power over the enemy.

When the gates and the walls were torn down or broken down, it gave access for the enemy to come in.

As mentioned earlier, there were city gates and there were temple gates.

Even as the Bible speaks of literal gates, the first gates we need to be keepers of are the gates of our very lives. We are the temple of the Holy Ghost.

We must protect what comes through our ear gates, our eye gates, our mouth gate, our nose gate and even the gate of our skin. We must be careful what we touch. We must also protect the gateway to our physical intimacy.

What are we watching on television? What kind of music are we listening to? What are we eating? We must protect the temple of God and then become those who protect our families, homes cities, states, and nations.

So, we are gatekeepers in the realm of the spirit.

One of my favorite scriptures is found in Proverbs 8:

> **34** Blessed is the man who listens to me, watching daily at my gates, watching at the posts of my door.
> **35** For whoever finds me finds life, and obtains favor from the Lord.

Are you watching daily at His gates?

A biblical gatekeeper is one who guards access to a place:

- A residence John 18:17
- The ark 1 Chronicles 15-16
- The temple 1 Chronicles 23:30-32
- The city Samuel 18:24; 2 Kings 7:10-11

The city gates were places of assembly. At the city gates, the elders conducted business and gathered there to make important decisions concerning the city and people. We need wise leadership in the church to guard and keep watch over God's people and seek God to make wise decisions.

The city gates were where the people assembled for social and legal matters to be settled. It was a place for marketing, business, reading and teaching the law. It was a place to attract the notice of the King and gain an audience with him. It was a place of authority and punishment and the place where the prophetic word came forth.

God has called us all to be keepers of spiritual gates. We must place ourselves at the gates of our home, our church, our city, and our nation.

Let us take our positions at the gates through prayer, intercession, dance, praise, worship and speaking the word of God.

Nehemiah is a book about restoration. It shows us that walls also act as gates and we must repair them with worship, intercession, and prayer.

The book of Nehemiah actually gives us a picture of Christ. It tells us the story of a man who had been placed by God as the cupbearer to the King, yet he gave up a high position to identify with the plight of his people.

At the time of Nehemiah, Jerusalem was the spiritual and political center of Judah. In chapter one, we read that his countrymen came to him to report that Nebuchadnezzar had destroyed the walls of Jerusalem and the gates had been burned with fire.

Nehemiah 1
> I asked them concerning the Jews who had escaped, who had survived the captivity, and concerning Jerusalem.

3 And they said to me, 'The survivors who are left from the captivity in the province are there in great distress and reproach. The wall of Jerusalem is also broken down, and its gates are burned with fire.

Without walls, it could hardly be considered a city. It was open to enemy attack and ungodly influences. Upon hearing this news, the Bible says that Nehemiah wept, fasted and prayed to the God of Heaven. After receiving permission to go to inspect the gates, he then called the people together to repair the gates that had been destroyed. Nehemiah went to Jerusalem and saw that the gates of protection and authority in his city were burned with fire.

May I suggest that many gates of the present-day church have been burned with fire yet many of us do not open our eyes to see the need or are not willing to do the work necessary for rebuilding. If we are to see God's prophetic destiny fulfilled, we must position ourselves at the gates.

In many churches, it is business as usual, Sunday after Sunday. However, our laziness, lethargy, selfishness, traditions, backbiting, jealousy, competitive spirit and sins have allowed our gates to be destroyed and left us vulnerable to enemy attacks.

We need to listen for God's voice, look and see in the spirit realm and be repairers of the gates in our own lives, our families, our churches and our nation.

What gates are in need of repair?

1. Let us repair the gates of a Holy walk with God so we can go forth to do His works in the earth.

2. Let us repair the gates of salvation for the harvest to come in.
3. Let us repair the gates of revelation and prophetic anointing with repentance, humility, and cleansing with God's word.

> *Let us come to the house of God with no agenda, other than to seek Him in order to see His will done in the earth as it is in heaven.*

In the Old Testament, we see that the priests washed, made sacrifices and were sanctified at the temple gates. I believe this also speaks of the local church. 2 Chronicles 31:2 says, The priests were appointed to stand and give thanks and praise "in the gates of the tents of the Lord."

As New Testament priests, we must learn to stand and give thanks and praise and offer spiritual sacrifices to our God. Let us come to the house of God with no agenda, other than to seek Him in order to see His will done in the earth as it is in heaven.

Let us cry out to Him and give way to Him. Let us yearn for that which is real, not that which is manufactured. Man cannot duplicate what God gives by His Spirit. Let us yearn to see God, to hear Him.

Because praise and worship is an entrance into the presence of God, it is a gate that is often in need of repair. Praise and worship establish the Kingdom of God in the earth. Let us empty our songs and make way for His songs. Let us empty our dances and make way for His dances.

God has a purpose for every time we gather together. Our culture breeds performance. We often see talent and call it the anointing. Let us become aware of the goings of God in the midst of

His people. It is not the job of praise and worship leaders to sing the latest songs. It is their job to lift the heavy burdens off of the people as they come into the Lord's house so they can be free to offer praise to God. It is their assignment to minister and sings over the people - to be lifters of burdens. Remember, "Psalmist are carriers of the words of God, musicians are carriers of the sounds of God and dancers are carriers of the sights of God." Let us be those words, sounds, and sights at the gates, that God may visit us in Spirit and in Truth, that we might see the gates of the church repaired.

In 2 Chronicles 23:19 the gatekeepers were in place so nothing unclean could enter in.

> **19** And he set the porters at the gates of the house of the LORD, that none which was unclean in anything should enter in.

We need to take our assigned positions and be the authority at the gates.

There were also gatekeepers at the temple treasuries and storehouses,

This is found in 1 Chronicles 9
> **26** For these Levites, the four chief porters were in
> their set office, and were over the chambers and treasuries of
> the house of God.
> **27** And they lodged round about the house of God, because the charge was upon them, and the opening thereof every morning pertained to them.

We are called to prophesy, decree, proclaim and speak God's word, sing His songs, release His sounds and dance over the lives of our families as well as ours. We cannot always go to the literal gates of a city but we can go in the spirit realm. Let us be responsible to minister at the gates through praise, worship, prayer, and intercession.

Where there are people of righteousness, praise and the prophetic word of God, the spiritual climate of a family, city or nation can be affected for God's purposes.

Even as in the days of Mordecai and Esther, God is positioning us at the gates in prayer so that He can expose the plans of the enemy and give us a strategy to overcome every time.

As we position ourselves at the gates, God will allow us to hear the plans of the enemy and show us how to overthrow anything that would try to stop us from advancing personally, corporately and nationally.

To close the gates of hell we must first open the gates of Heaven. Light overcomes darkness. As the revelation of His will is revealed, we will certainly overthrow Haman and his sons! Every diabolical plot that the enemy tries to form against us will be rerouted and will boomerang back upon his own head!

Prophesy at the gates that no weapon formed against us will prosper!

Let's be watchmen at the gates. Then we will be prepared and ready to take back our land.

A watchman is one who leans forward to peer into the distance. A watchman will worship, listen, observe and wait on the strategies of God to be revealed.

The watchman would always say what he saw.

Isaiah 21

6 The Lord said, go set a watchman, let him declare (announce) what he sees.

You must see and say according to the word of God and the promises He has made over your life and over your nation.

Allow God to set you as a watchman for your nation. Cry out to Him and put Him in remembrance of His word as it pertains to His promises for your nation. Fast and pray for divine strategies to see the foundation of your land and your nation restored and established in righteousness. Remember, you have the power and the authority!

Luke 10

19 Behold, I give unto you power to tread on serpents and scorpions, and over all the power of the enemy: and nothing shall by any means hurt you.

Ephesians 3

20 Now unto him, that is able to do exceeding abundantly above all that we ask or think, according to the power (Dunamis) that worketh in us,

It is time for the Bride of Christ in every nation to arise in worship. Restoration of our land will not take place without the worship of the ekklesia.

In a kingdom, worship is required. We cannot be in His kingdom and not worship. Kingdom worship is not a dance, it's not music, it's not a concert or a song service. It is about releasing the power and authority given to us by God to bring the presence of the King in the earth realm.

Worship is what brings the presence of the Lord. Every song, every sound, every move must be with dunamis and exousia for the purpose of bringing God's kingdom here in this nation.

Worship should not be reserved for a Sunday service or a special gathering. Worship is not a religious act, it is a supernatural kingdom power. It is also a personal and national expression of gratitude and a key to seeing God's power released in any nation.

Gratitude is the highest form of worship. Men can be respected and honored but we must never worship them. Worship is reserved only for kings. There is an urgent need for national worship. National worship is our responsibility and obligation. Nations must understand this powerful truth.

Why? Because God commanded that entire nations worship Him, not just a group of people within the nation.

Pray for the government of your nation to initiate true thanksgiving and worship. That is God's strategy for building a nation and bringing His redemptive purposes to pass.

His first commandment dealt with worship and idolatry. He alone is God. He alone is worthy.

Exodus 20

3 Thou shalt have no other gods before me.

4 Thou shalt not make unto thee any graven image or any likeness of anything that is in heaven above, or that is in the earth beneath, or that is in the water under the earth:

God told Pharaoh to let His people go so they could worship Him.

Exodus 5
> **1** And afterward, Moses and Aaron went in, and told Pharaoh, Thus saith the LORD God of Israel, Let my people go, that they may hold a feast unto me in the wilderness.

Feast is the word Chagag, meaning to move in a circle, i.e. (specifically) to march in a sacred procession, to observe a festival; by implication, to be giddy, to celebrate, to dance.

God's desire for the nation of Israel was for them to worship, which would result in economic and social changes for the nation. The entire nation was called to worship. Every man, woman, and child was called to worship. Therefore, corporate worship was equally as important as individual worship. This still holds true for us today.

Individual worship protects us when we acknowledge that God owns everything. Individual gratitude protects us

In the same way, national worship and national gratitude guarantees that the nation will prosper

When a nation honors God, He guarantees His protection. That's why it is important for nations to worship. There is a Kingdom culture of worship and we must be about bringing that kingdom culture to our nation.

Remember the dominion mandate of Genesis 1:
> **26** Then God said, "Let Us make man in Our image, according to Our likeness; let them have dominion over the fish of the sea, over the birds of the air, and over the cattle, over all the earth and over every creeping thing that creeps on the earth."

Dr. Myles Munroe states that God's original plan was for "Him to rule in heaven and for us to rule on the earth."

Psalm 115

16 The heaven, even the heavens, are the Lord's; but the earth hath He given to the children of men.

God rules in heaven, we rule in earth. Know that we have Dunamis and Exousia for the purpose of ruling in the earth. We are not helpless! We are not victims. We are victors!

Whatever God says about our nation, we must say. Our words are spirit and life when we say what He says.

We are seated with Him. Therefore, we can speak from the throne. We speak from a position of authority and power.

Psalm 149

6 Let the high praises of God be in their mouth, and a two-edged sword in their hand;

7 To execute vengeance upon the heathen, and punishments upon the people;

8 To bind their kings with chains, and their nobles with fetters of iron;

9 To execute upon them the judgment written: this honour have all his saints

From there, we become the judicial system of heaven legislating in the earth on behalf of heaven. I will discuss this more in the next chapter.

We must speak as kings in the earth. We do not have to bow to the Babylonian system. Kings do not question their authority. We must know that we are kings in the earth and operate in kingly authority

We are seated with Him in heavenly places so we have throne room authority. I am a king as well as a priest. We are kingly in our authority and priestly in our worship. It's time to understand the power of worship and connect it to the prophetic destiny of our nation! This is how we graduate from contending for the promises to apprehending His promises.

The Lordship of the king is tied to his territory.

2 Chronicles 7
14 If my people, which are called by my name, shall humble themselves, and pray, and seek my face, and turn from their wicked ways; then will I hear from heaven, and will forgive their sin, and will heal their land.

In every nation, our land needs healing. We have a covenantal relationship with the land. As gatekeepers and watchmen, we must repent for the sin and iniquity of the land.

We are one with the land because that is where we came from.

Genesis 2:7 tells us that we came from the ground, from the land. We are dust. God even used the land against His enemies. He used dust as a weapon.

Exodus 8
16 And the LORD said unto Moses, say unto Aaron, stretch out thy rod, and smite the dust of the land, that it may become lice throughout all the land of Egypt.
17 And they did so; for Aaron stretched out his hand with his rod,

and smote the dust of the earth, and it became lice in man, and in beast; all the dust of the land became lice throughout all the land of Egypt.

We are one with the land because we live in the land. It is our assigned dwelling place. Therefore, we have a daily connection with the land.

The earth has a mouth.

Genesis 4
9 And the LORD said unto Cain, where is Abel thy brother? And he said, I know not: Am I my brother's keeper?
10 And he said, What hast thou done? the voice of thy brother's blood crieth unto me from the ground.
11 And now art thou cursed from the earth, which hath opened her mouth to receive thy brother's blood from thy hand;
The land has a soul. The land can hear!

Jeremiah 6
19 Hear, O earth: behold, I am bringing disaster on this people, The fruit of their plans, Because they have not listened to My words, And as for My law, they have rejected it also.

Micah 1
2 Hear, O peoples, all of you; Listen, O earth and all it contains, And let the Lord GOD be a witness against you, The Lord from His holy temple.

We can also speak life to the land because we are one with the land.

Ezekiel 37

4 Again He said to me, "Prophesy over these bones and say to them, 'O dry bones, hear the word of the LORD.

We need to ask God for His new strategies on how to take and possess the land. The land does not sleep. It hears and responds based on what we say.

May the land rise and fight back for us against our enemies!

God is the Lord of the armies. The land is part of the army God has given us to fight with. We must learn to summons the land as a weapon of warfare

> *We need to ask God for His new strategies on how to take and possess the land. The land does not sleep. It hears and responds based on what we say.*

Let us raise altars of worship to the Lord God on the land. Speak to the land. Walk through the land. It is where the souls of our feet tread that God has given us to possess.

Whatever land you have been promised as part of your inheritance, go walk upon it!

Numbers 16

30 But if the LORD make a new thing, and the earth opens her mouth, and swallow them up, with all that appertain unto them, and they go down quick into the pit; then ye shall understand that these men have provoked the LORD.

31 And it came to pass, as he had made an end of speaking all these words, that the ground clave asunder that was under them:

32 And the earth opened her mouth and swallowed them up, and their houses, and all the men that appertained unto Korah, and all their goods.

33 They and all that appertained to them went down alive into the pit, and the earth closed upon them: and they perished from among the congregation.

34 And all Israel that were round about them fled at the cry of them: for they said, Lest the earth swallow us up also.

As a prophetic watchman, the destiny of your nation is in your hands but God has the strategy. Listen to heaven, then declare it in the earth.

The dominion in the earth is still ours until He comes to bring His dominion in the earth and the kingdoms of the world become the kingdom of our Lord and of His Christ. (Revelation 11:15)

The devil is illegal in the land! Jesus came and destroyed the work of the evil one. 1 John 3:8

Jesus made a show of him openly, triumphing over him! Colossians 2:15

Isaiah 34

1 Come near, ye nations, to hear; and hearken ye people: let the earth hear, and all that is therein; the world, and all things that come forth of it.

Since the earth, the land can hear, we must speak! Oh earth, open your mouth and swallow every conspiracy against my life and against my nation. Land, we are in covenant. Rise up and fight with us! Let the land receive you and rejoice!

Job 5

23 For thou shalt be in league with the stones of the field: make a covenant with the land.

Let us make decrees over the land, both in our homeland and even when we travel to other nations!

I decree that the land will not fight against me!

I decree that the land shall favor me!

Because I am a prophetic watchman, the land shall hear my voice and love me and prosper me and work for me!

(Say the name of your nation) ...you shall love me, you will favor me, you shall never reject me, you shall celebrate me as I worship the King of kings.

The land must also be cleansed. If the land is not cleansed, it will continue to breed negative or unhealthy practices that may have been taking place in the land for years.

We are stewards of our land. We are the gatekeepers. We are the prophetic watchmen.

Prophetic demonstrations for the gates. Let's enter His gates with thanksgiving and His courts with praise. Take time to sing and/or dance the following scriptures over your nation.

Let's use the authority God has given us, take our positions at the gates and become visual demonstration of what God is saying and doing to release His plans into the earth.

Our feet represent authority and He has said He would give us every piece of ground our feet tread upon. Joshua 1:3
He has given us the necks of our enemies (Psalm 18:40) and makes the enemy like ashes under the souls of our feet. Malachi 4:3

Our hands also represent authority. We raise them to God in surrender and we clap them unto our God in praise. We also clap them together to smite the enemy. The enemy knows the difference in a clap of praise and one that is intended as a weapon of our warfare.

We shout unto God with a voice of triumph! We shout because the enemy is defeated, not to defeat him. Jesus has already accomplished that on our behalf according to Colossians 2:15.

Hosea 2

21 And it shall come to pass in that day, I will hear, (speak, respond, bear witness) saith the LORD, I will hear the heavens, and they shall hear the earth;
22 And the earth shall hear the corn, (increase) and the (new) wine, and the oil (anointing) and they shall hear Jezreel. (God will sow)
23 And I will sow her unto me in the **earth**, and I will have mercy upon her that had not obtained mercy; and I will say to them which

were not my people, Thou art my people; and they shall say, Thou art my God.

Victory is ours if we will only take our positions as prophetic watchmen at the gates.

ACTION

Pray, decree, sing and /or dance with these words:
Father in Heaven, I come to you in the name of Jesus, and I take my position at the gate of this temple in which you dwell.

Forgive me for not taking my position at the gates daily and for not always protecting your temple.

Now that I know this spiritual truth, I will be a gatekeeper of your temple. My body is the temple of the Holy Spirit. In you, I live and move and have my being.

My eyes are yours. My ears are yours.

I surrender to you all that I take in through my mouth gate and my gate to physical intimacy.

Make me more sensitive to you Holy Spirit.

Lead me and guide me. Work in me a heart to obey you.

Father, show me how to be a gatekeeper for my family, my neighborhood, my church, my city, my state, my nation and even other nations.

Allow me to be one who repairs the gates so that others may know you. As I take my position at the gate, reveal your strategies to me so I can complete your assignment for me in the earth.

10 ARISE, DANCE AND LEGISLATE

Jesus preached about the kingdom. When Jesus came He brought a kingdom, not a dead religion with no power. His desire was to establish the kingdom the hearts of men. The kingdom is about returning the governing authority of God in the earth.
God wants us to learn how to live and function in that authority

"A kingdom is the sovereign impact, influence, and ruler-ship of a King over a territory and a people impacting it with His will, His intent and His purpose." Dr. Myles Munroe

Every kingdom has a government.

Isaiah 9

> *6 For unto us a child is born, unto us a son is given: and the government shall be upon his shoulder: and his name shall be called Wonderful, Counsellor, The mighty God, The everlasting Father, The Prince of Peace.*
>
> *7 Of the increase of his government and peace there shall be no end, upon the throne of David, and upon his kingdom, to order it, and to establish it with judgment and with justice from henceforth even forever. The zeal of the LORD of hosts will perform this.*

Government is the word Misrah. It is the foundation of all government, even in the earth today. The government of God is about establishing the rule, reign, and order of God.

What is a government? A government is an authority that impacts a territory. Every government has ambassadors that represent them.

We are ambassadors. Ambassadors are given power and authority from the government that they represent.

Ambassadors represent the government but they never live in the country they represent. That's where we come in!

Our government in heaven has sent us here into the earth realm to represent the government of heaven here on earth. The Misrah anointing is being released in the earth to kingdom citizens. You are not just a citizen of whatever nation you were born in.

Everywhere we go, we go as ambassadors of a heavenly government.

Remember Genesis 1.

26 Then God said," Let us make man in our image, according to our likeness; let them have dominion..."

Dominion is the power to manage, control, lead, rule and have authority over.

Image means the way God thinks...it has to do with His character.

Likeness means the way God expresses Himself.

Dominion means the way God acts.

We are to think as God thinks. We are to have the same mind as Christ Jesus. So, thinking as God thinks is possible!

We are also called to rule in this life with the authority of the king.

The first Adam lost the government of God. The second Adam came to restore this governmental authority. The prefix re means to put back in its original state.

Every kingdom has a culture. Our culture is found in the fruit of the Spirit - love, joy, peace, long-suffering, gentleness, faith, meekness, temperance, unity, serving, humility and preferring one another.

Every kingdom has a constitution to tell us our rights and privileges. The constitution tells us about the laws of the kingdom.

The Constitution of our government tells us in Matthew 28 about the authority God has entrusted to His Ambassadors.

Matthew 28

18 All authority has been given to Me in heaven and on earth.

> *You have been sent from heaven to your nation to have the authority of the king.*

The word authority means power, ability, privilege, influence, liberty, lawful jurisdiction.

All authority has been given to us! How much authority? All authority. Heaven lets us know that our authority knows no boundaries. We are not bound by any territorial jurisdiction.

We have authority in every nation.

From the Caribbean to Asia, from Africa to South America!

You have been sent from heaven to your nation to have the authority of the king. We have been mantled with this authority to represent the government of heaven on earth.

A mantle represents authority. A mantle gives you the right to exercise certain duties. A mantle is your assignment from God with delegated, corresponding authority to fulfill it. So, our authority is in direct proportion to the One who gives the authority.

Matthew 16

13 When Jesus came into the coasts of Caesarea Philippi, he asked his disciples, saying, Whom do men say that I the Son of man am?
14 And they said Some say that thou art John the Baptist: some, Elias; and others, Jeremias, or one of the prophets.
15 He saith unto them, But whom say ye that I am?
16 And Simon Peter answered and said, Thou art the Christ, the Son of the living God.
17 And Jesus answered and said unto him, Blessed art thou, Simon Barjona: for flesh and blood hath not revealed it unto thee, but my Father which is in heaven.
18 And I say also unto thee, That thou art Peter, and upon this rock, I will build my church (ecclesia); and the gates of hell shall not prevail against it.
19 And I will give unto thee the keys of the kingdom of heaven: and whatsoever thou shalt bind on earth shall be bound in heaven: and whatsoever thou shalt loose on earth shall be loosed in heaven.

As mentioned earlier, the word church is the word Ecclesia. It is not a religious term. It is a governmental term. Ecclesia mentioned in context of the kingdom. Ecclesia means called out ones. Those chosen to be in a government cabinet or Senate. The function of the ecclesia is to know the mind of king, the intent of king, the heart of king, the purposes of the king and turn it into legislation on earth.

You are a government official so you must learn to think governmentally.

It is time for a new wineskin - new ways of thinking. We must have a paradigm shift!

God has given you the keys. Keys represent power, authority, and access. Keys are used to lock and unlock. Your enemy does not want you to know you have keys. If he can't keep you out of church, he will try to deceive you while you are in the church.

The Bible filled with keys. Here are a few examples.

Deuteronomy 28 reads as follows:
1 And it shall come to pass, if thou shalt hearken diligently unto the voice of the LORD thy God, to observe and to do all his commandments which I command thee this day, that the LORD thy God will set thee on high above all nations of the earth:
2 And all these blessings shall come on thee, and overtake thee if thou shalt hearken unto the voice of the LORD thy God.
3 Blessed shalt thou be in the city, and blessed shalt thou be in the field.
4 Blessed shall be the fruit of thy body, and the fruit of thy ground, and the fruit of thy cattle, the increase of thy kind, and the flocks of thy sheep.
5 Blessed shall be thy basket and thy store.
6 Blessed shalt thou be when thou comest in, and blessed shalt thou be when thou goest out.
7 The LORD shall cause thine enemies that rise up against thee to Be smitten before thy face: they shall come out against thee one way, and flee before thee seven ways
8 The LORD shall command the blessing upon thee in thy storehouses, and in all that thou settest thine hand unto, and he shall bless thee in the land which the LORD thy God giveth thee.

9 The LORD shall establish thee a holy people unto himself, as he hath sworn unto thee if thou shalt keep the commandments of the LORD thy God, and walk in his ways.

10 And all people of the earth shall see that thou art called by the name of the LORD; and they shall be afraid of thee.

11 And the LORD shall make thee plenteous in goods, in the fruit of thy body, and in the fruit of thy cattle, and in the fruit f thy ground, in the land which the LORD sware unto thy fathers to give thee.

12 The LORD shall open unto thee his good treasure, the heaven to give the rain unto thy land in his season, and to bless all the work of thine hand: and thou shalt lend unto many nations, and thou shalt not borrow.

13 And the LORD shall make thee the head, and not the tail, and thou shalt be above only, and thou shalt not be beneath; if that thou hearkens unto the commandments of the LORD thy God, which I command thee this day, to observe and to do them:

14 And thou shalt not go aside from any of the words which I command thee this day, to the right hand, or to the left, to go after other gods to serve them.

To hearken diligently means to obey! What a powerful key! Obedience leads to many blessings! Use your key of obedience! Bind the spirit of disobedience.

Tithing is a key found in Malachi 3.

10 Bring ye all the tithes into the storehouse, that there may be meat in mine house, and prove me now herewith, saith the LORD of hosts, if I will not open you the windows of heaven, and pour you out a blessing, that there shall not be room enough to receive it.

11 And I will rebuke the devourer for your sakes, and he shall not destroy the fruits of your ground; neither shall your vine cast her fruit before the time in the field, saith the LORD of hosts.

12 And all nations shall call you blessed: for ye shall be a delightsome land, saith the LORD of hosts.

Tithing keeps the windows of heaven open, and causes God to rebuke anything that would come to try to devour you.

Another key is found in Luke Chapter 6.

38 Give, and it shall be given unto you; good measure, pressed down, and shaken together, and running over, shall men give into your bosom. For with the same measure that ye mete withal, it shall be measured to you again.

Again, we see a powerful key that we can use! Giving will cause men to give to you! Use your keys!

As the ecclesia of God, what are you supposed to be doing?

Let's look at Mark 16.

15 And he said unto them, Go ye into all the world, and preach the gospel to every creature.

17 And these signs shall follow them that believe; In my name shall they cast out devils; they shall speak with new tongues;

18 They shall take up serpents; and if they drink any deadly thing, it shall not hurt them; they shall lay hands on the sick, and they shall recover.

Ecclesia has to do with governing.
In an army, the general has all the authority. A private has none.

When does the private have the same authority as the general? When the general sends the private on a special mission or a special assignment in his name. The private is then free to use the name and the authority of the general.

God is the general and we are the privates but we have been sent by the general so we have the authority of the general!

We have learned about religion and about how to "do" church but not how to be the ecclesia. We now need to learn the true meaning of the word ecclesia.

As the governing body of Christ, we are called to:
- Have a dominion mandate
- Disciple nations
- Make earth look like God's kingdom
- Submit to Jesus as our apostle and commander
- Decree according to the laws of God
- Worship with prophetic revelation
- Access all the resources of the throne
- Be the voice of the King in the earth
- Grow up in our gifts and calling
- Allow Holy Spirit to lead us as sons of God
- Focus on expanding the kingdom.
- Understand that we have the mandate to save and heal nations
- Understand that we have authority to deal with the nations
- Know our kingdom purpose and help others find their purpose
- Live in mandatory obedience

- Rule in the midst of our enemies
- Create what comes, not just take what comes
- Be strong warriors who enforce the victory Jesus already won for us

2 Timothy

3 Thou, therefore, endure hardness, as a good soldier of Jesus Christ.
4 No man that warreth entangleth himself with the affairs of this life; that he may please him who hath chosen him to be a soldier.

1 John 3

8 For this purpose, the Son of God was manifested, that he might destroy the works of the devil.

He destroyed the works of the enemy! Now we enforce everything He won for us!

We must know that we are kings in the earth and operate ours in kingly authority. We must speak as kings. Kings do not question their authority. They know that they were born to rule.

KINGS! Rise up and come out of hiding!

When a king speaks, a transformation takes place in the atmosphere because the word of a king becomes law.

As the ecclesia of God, we are destroyers of all darkness. We tear down strongholds and bring down principalities over regions and nations. We are as bold as lions.

Ecclesia arises and goes beyond the four walls of a church building. Become the ecclesia. The Misrah anointing is in the earth. Understanding this gives you the power to legislate.

Job 22
28 Thou shall decree a thing and it shall be established unto thee and the light shall shine upon thy ways

A decree is an official order issued by a legal authority. It is a judicial decision. To "decree a thing" means to decree His promises.

What has God said to you?

Decree it and it shall be established or accomplished. Then, light shall shine and illumination will come to guide you on His paths. You will be able to see where you are going!

As the ecclesia, called to Legislate, our function is to perform the function of legislation, specifically to make or enact laws. We mandate, establish and regulate everything within our sphere through legislation.

To legislate means to make laws. God's word is His law. So, we legislate according to God's word.

God's Word says healing belongs to us! Once when I was experiencing pain in my legs, I began to legislate healing according to the Word of God, I laid hands on myself and the pain disappeared.

The Word of God also promises peace. On a recent fight, it was evident by the sound of a crying child that my flight might not be a peaceful flight. Without moving from my seat, I began to speak and legislate peace for the crying child. Within a minute or so, the crying stopped and we all had a peaceful flight. Glory to God!

Joshua 1

>**8** This book of the Law shall not depart from your mouth, but you shall meditate in it day and night, that you may observe to do according to all that is written in it. For then you will make your way prosperous, and then you will have good success.

Just as God established physical laws, such as the law of gravity, so there are spiritual laws that have been set in motion by God and they are just as sure as physical laws.

Physical laws can be found in a physics book. Spiritual laws can be found in the Word of God.

Every day we get up and get out of bed and never think about most of these natural laws that rule our lives. Yet they affect what we do regardless of whether we are thinking of them or not.

The law of gravity, the law of motion, the laws of thermodynamics and the laws of aerodynamics are just a few of these scientific systems that we depend upon. You may or may not understand how these laws work, yet you use them and they work for your good.

If you want to go to California from New York, the law of aerodynamics can help your pilot override the laws of gravity and help you to get to your destination in a matter of a few hours.

God and His kingdom operate under a set of strict spiritual laws that we need to understand.

1. **Romans 3**

    27 Where is boasting then? It is excluded. By what law? of works? Nay: but by the law of faith.

Faith is a spiritual law. The just shall live by...faith! Romans 1:17

2. **Romans 8**

    2 For the law of spirit of life in Christ Jesus has made me free from the law of sin and death.

Here we see two opposing laws – the law of Life in Christ Jesus has superseded the law of sin and death. These are two principles based upon the natural law of cause and effect.

The result of sin is death. That is a law that cannot be revoked or reversed. But being born again and embracing the law of the Spirit of Life in Christ Jesus, we overcome the law of sin and death. So even when we die, we still live!

3. **Galatians 6**

    7 Be not deceived; God is not mocked: for whatsoever a man soweth, that shall he also reaps.

This gives us a clear picture of a spiritual law that governs our lives every day. Sowing and reaping is a spiritual law. It affects everyone equally, whether they realize it or not.

Even farmers understand the law of sowing and reaping. They plant specific seeds to get specific crops and harvests. They do not plant corn seed to get cabbage. They understand that whatever they sow, is exactly what they reap. This is a spiritual law as well as a natural physical law.

Genesis 8
>22 While the earth remaineth, seedtime and harvest, and cold and heat, and summer and winter, and day and night shall not cease.

So, the function of the ecclesia is to legislate - make laws according to the
Word of God, thereby bringing the will of God into the earth.

Proverbs 18:21 tells us that "Death and life are in the power of the tongue. 'That's a spiritual law. Whatever you are saying is what you are legislating, either life in accordance to the Word of God or death which is not in accordance to the word of God.

You have what you say. Speak His word. That is how you legislate. Then God can watch over His word to perform it, Jeremiah 1:12.

Psalm 149
>6 Let the high praises of God be in their mouth, and a two-edged sword in their hand;
>7 To execute vengeance upon the heathen and punishments upon the people;
>8 To bind their kings with chains, and their nobles with fetters of iron;
>9 To execute upon them the judgment written: this honor have all his saints. Praise ye the LORD.

The function of the ecclesia is to execute the judgment written! It is written….

1 John 4
4 Ye are of God little children, and have overcome them because greater is he that is in you, than he that is in the world.

Isaiah 54
17 No weapon that is formed against thee shall prosper and every tongue that shall rise against thee in judgment thou shalt condemn. This is the heritage of the servants of the LORD, and their righteousness is of me, saith the LORD.

Isaiah 40
31 But they that wait upon the LORD shall renew their strength; they shall mount up with wings as eagles; they shall run, and not be weary, and they shall walk, and not faint.

Why do you need the Misrah anointing? It puts you in God zone, speaking the Word God, bringing the kingdom to earth.

What we hear from heaven, we must speak into the earth. Then we become the judicial system of heaven legislating in the earth on behalf of heaven.

Arise and legislate!

ACTION

Based on what you need to see God do in your life, take the word of God and begin to legislate as you dance over each promise God has made to you.

11 GLOBAL IMPACT DANCING IN HIS GLORY

I was made for glory. You were made for glory. It is a gift from God. Glory is the inheritance of every believer.

The word glory is defined as weight, splendor, copiousness, honor or honorable. Only God has true glory. His glory shines brighter than the sun.

But Psalm 8 tells us that we are crowned with glory, therefore, we are created to live in the glory of our God - to walk in the glory, talk in the glory, dance in the glory of our God.

1 A Psalm of David. O LORD our Lord, how excellent is thy name in all the earth! Who hast set thy glory above the heavens.

2 Out of the mouth of babes and sucklings, hast thou ordained strength because of thine enemies, that thou mightest still the enemy and the avenger.
3 When I consider thy heavens, the work of thy fingers, the moon and the stars, which thou hast ordained;
4 What is man, that thou art mindful of him? and the son of man, that thou visitest him?
5 For thou hast made him a little lower than the angels, and hast crowned him with glory and honour.
6 Thou madest him to have dominion over the works of thy hands; thou hast put all things under his feet:
9 O LORD our Lord, how excellent is thy name in all the earth!

Looking at the story of Psalm 8, David kept his father's sheep. As a young man, he was with his sheep day night. I believe that as David saw the moon and the stars, he came to know God. Therefore, he knew that the strong and powerful God made them all.

David also knew that the enemies of God were against Him and His people. Through His intimate relationship with God and revelation of God's power, he knew that God would fight for His people and make His people strong. God is more powerful than all his enemies. God will always win.

Sometimes the power and grace of God appear wonderfully in those who are most unlikely to rule. Sometimes the power of God brings to pass great things by very weak and unlikely instruments, that the excellency of the power might more evidently appear to be of God, and not of man. When these unlikely instruments conquer the most powerful and malicious enemies, it confounds them, and advances the glory of God.

Strength, force, security, majesty, praise, boldness, might and power has been ordained. This He does, because of His enemies, that He may put them to silence.

The majesty and glory of our King make us want to glorify Him. There are no words that can truly express His excellent greatness. Let us shout aloud with the words of David, "O LORD our Lord, how excellent is thy name in all the earth!"

His name is powerful, mighty, noble, worthy, great and magnificent! His name is glorious and honorable. Yet, He, the Almighty Sovereign King, sees us, cares for us and, yes! He remembers us and visits us.

God created man for His glory. Isaiah 43: 7 says, "Even every one that is called by My name: for I have created him for My glory, I have formed him; yea, I have made him."

We were created for His glory. We live, move and have our being in His glory. God makes the minister and the ministry one.

Therefore, every part of our lives is meant to be surrounded, enveloped and crowned with His glory.

We are encircled and compassed about, both when we are attacked by the enemies of our soul and when we need protection.

This is the revelation we must learn and live in to manifest the glory of God that will change hearts and ultimately, change nations.

God has crowned us with glory and honor. The word honor means magnificence, splendor, beauty, comeliness, excellency, majesty and favor.

This same God has made us to have dominion over the works of His hands.

Dominion means to rule, to govern, to reign and to cause to have power. He has caused us to have power.

He has put all things under our feet. Psalm 91 tells us that because the Lord is our habitation, He gives His angels charge over us and causes us to tread upon the lion and adder - upon the young lion and the dragon.

Those things that try to oppress us will be overtaken by the glory, and our feet, then become the oppressor of our enemies. Through our dance, we trample our enemies under our feet.

We dance through troops - those things that try to press against us - and we leap over walls.

He makes our feet like hinds 'feet, enlarges our steps under us and makes sure that our feet do not slip, shake or slide so we can be carriers of His glory.

Our enemies fall under our feet. He gives us strength for the battle and subdues under us those that rise up against us.

He has also given us the necks of our enemies to dance upon injustice and upon those that desire our destruction.

As we dance in the glory, we take salvation to the nations.

Romans 10
13 For whosoever shall call upon the name of the Lord shall be saved.

14 How then shall they call on him in whom they have not believed? and how shall they believe in him of whom they have not heard? and how shall they hear without a preacher?
15 And how shall they preach, except they be sent? As it is written, how beautiful are the feet of them that preach the gospel of peace, and bring glad tidings of good things.

As we dance, our feet preach the gospel of peace. Our feet dance tidings of good things. Wherever our feet trod, we carry the presence and the glory of God. This is how the glory of our God will cover the earth as the waters cover the sea.

Our dance can create an atmosphere for the glory of His presence to manifest. Through our worship, we build a throne for the King.

The highest form of worship is when we become worship, not just do worship through the dance.

Our lives must reflect the king. As we die to ourselves, we can begin to hear from heaven and dance the dances that He releases from His heart and from His throne.

Until then, we have not begun to dance in the glory.

Because we were created to worship, we do not lean to our own understanding but we yield our bodies to God as living sacrifices and allow Him to dance His dances through us.

Just as the keys on a keyboard do not move unless someone plays the keys, so we can yield to Holy Spirit and allow Him to play us like an instrument.
Once we are yielded instruments, He can release His glory.

In the glory, there is no lack. Healing, deliverance, joy, salvation, provision will all be released as we dance in the glory. Our regions will be transformed as we dance in the glory.

His glory shifts and transforms people, places, and things.

To walk, live, dance in the glory of God means to administrate His government and His kingdom in the earth realm.

We must remember that the ultimate focus in worship is the presence of the Lord, not our physical activities. Worship must focus on Him, not on self. Let us cry out for that which is authentic so we do not fill our worship with mere physical activities.

Psalms 96

6 Honour and majesty are before him: strength and beauty are in his sanctuary.
7 Give unto the LORD, O ye kindreds of the people, give unto the LORD glory and strength.
8 Give unto the LORD the glory due unto his name: bring an offering, and come into his courts.
9 O worship the LORD in the beauty of holiness: fear...twist or whirl in a circular or spiral manner, - dance before him, all the earth.
10 Say among the heathen that the LORD reigneth: the world also shall be established that it shall not be moved: he shall judge the people righteously.

Rejoice! Jump for joy! God has turned our mourning into dancing! He has put off our sackcloth, and girded us with gladness! Our glory will sing praise to Him, and not be silent. We will not hold our peace.

As we surrender to the glory of the King, the impact will be felt globally.

I traveled to Korea and 30 days later, I traveled to Haiti. The two nations could not have been more different, yet both nations are in need of an impact of God's glory. I found the church in Korea to be alive, filled with joy and expectation, ready to impact their nation with God's glory. In vivid contrast, I experienced many people in Haiti who seemed to be in the middle of a spiritual hurricane as much as still recovering from the dramatic trauma of a natural hurricane.

The nations are in a tumultuous place. Let us dance in Haiti until the stronghold of voodoo is broken and the Body of Christ rises up in the splendor of the Lord.

Pray for indigenous people to rise up in righteousness. Then go forth and dance in Israel until the veils are removed from their eyes. Dance before the Lord and give Him no rest, until He establishes and makes Jerusalem a praise in the earth.

Dance in Holland until righteousness overtakes the land and the ladies of the red-light district realize that they were created by a loving God who sees their value and their worth.

Dance in South Africa until every remnant of apartheid is completely destroyed.

Dance in Mexico until every gang member and drug lord is converted and delivered from the kingdom of darkness to the kingdom of light.

Dance in the glory until wicked governments are brought down and people rejoice because the righteous become rulers.

Dance in every nation until the glory of God fills every kindred, and tongue and people.

Dance in the glory until the kingdoms of this world become the kingdoms of our Lord, and of his Christ. He shall reign forever and ever.

He is the King of glory! Let us glory in His holy name. Dance in His holy name so shall the heart of the nations rejoice as they seek the Lord.

Dance before Him in glory. Ascribe to Him, bring to Him the glory that is due His name and dance, all the earth. His kingdom will be established and His righteousness shall be released.

1 Chronicles 16

27 Glory and honour are in his presence; strength and gladness are in his place.
28 Give unto the LORD, ye kindreds of the people, give unto the LORD glory and strength.
29 Give unto the LORD the glory due unto his name: bring an offering, and come before him: worship the LORD in the beauty of holiness.
30 Fear before him, all the earth: the world also shall be stable, that it be not moved.

31 Let the heavens be glad, and let the earth rejoice: and let men say among the nations, The LORD reigneth.

First, we are told that glory is in His presence. Then, the scripture admonishes us to give, ascribe or bring Him glory. We are to bring an offering as we fall down and worship Him.

The first word in verse 30 is very interesting. The word fear is the word chuwl. It translates as "to twist or whirl in a circular manner, specifically to dance."

Can it be that all the physical earth was created to whirl before the Lord, thereby bringing glory to His name, establishing and stabilizing the inhabitants of the nations?

The same word can also be found in Psalms 90.

> **2** Before the mountains were brought forth, or ever thou hadst formed (chuwl) the earth and the world, even from everlasting to everlasting, thou art God.

Can it be that God Himself whirled in a circular manner as in dancing as He created the earth and the inhabitants thereof?

You will find this same word, chuwl, in Psalms 29.
> **2** Give unto the LORD the glory due unto his name; worship the LORD in the beauty of holiness.
> **3** The voice of the LORD is upon the waters: the God of glory thundereth: the LORD is upon many waters.
> **4** The voice of the LORD is powerful; the voice of the LORD is full of majesty.

5 The voice of the LORD breaketh the cedars; yea, the LORD breaketh the cedars of Lebanon.
6 He maketh them also to skip like a calf; Lebanon and Sirion like a young unicorn.
7 The voice of the LORD divideth the flames of fire.
8 The voice of the LORD shaketh the wilderness; the LORD shaketh the wilderness of Kadesh.
9 The voice of the LORD shaketh (chuwl) the wilderness; the LORD shaketh the wilderness of Kadesh.

> *As we worship in the beauty of holiness, this releases the majestic voice of the Lord and brings glory to our dance.*

As we worship in the beauty of holiness, this releases the majestic voice of the Lord and brings glory to our dance. Flames of fire attend the voice of God, illuminating our hearts, releasing His glory a holy flame. His voice is filled with glory and has the ability to dance over our wilderness, breaking down barriers and causing us to jump and leap wildly for joy.

John 17

22 And the glory which thou gave me I have given them; that they may be one, even as we are one:

He has given us His glory to make us one. We need the Glory to be one!

When we worship as one, Psalm 22 says He inhabits the praises of His people. He sets up His throne in the midst of our worship as He comes as judge.

When we worship as one, that's when the worship on earth reflects the worship in heaven.

As we worship as one, His judgment is released against our enemies! Oh Lord, our Lord, how excellent is Your name in all the earth!

His spiritual weight is His essence, His character, that which makes Him infinite and boundless, with no restrictions, has been given to us to be physical demonstrations of God's glory.

Isaiah 60

1 Arise, shine; for thy light is come, and the glory of the LORD is risen upon thee.
2 For, behold, the darkness shall cover the earth, and gross darkness the people: but the LORD shall arise upon thee, and his glory shall be seen upon thee.
3 And the Gentiles shall come to thy light, and kings to the brightness of thy rising.
4 Lift up thine eyes round about, and see: all they gather themselves together, they come to thee: thy sons shall come from far, and thy daughters shall be nursed at thy side.
5 Then thou shalt see, and flow together, and thine heart shall fear, and be enlarged; because the abundance of the sea shall be converted unto thee, the forces of the Gentiles shall come unto thee.

Arise is a call to stand up! Stir yourself! Shine! Be set on fire!

No more movement for the sake of movement. It is time for you to dance your prophetic destiny and see it manifest in the earth.

The call from heaven is to those who are willing to dance only for the purpose of releasing His glory! As you valiantly dance the dances of heaven, may His glory be seen upon you as a visible manifestation.

Heal the broken hearted, dance deliverance to the captives, open the prison doors with the key of God's glory. May nations be transformed by the brightness of your rising.

The world will know whose who carry His glory. They are waiting for the appearing, the coming, the illumination, the manifestation and revealed revelation of the sons of God. Dancing valiantly in the spirit, in the glory of God can have a global impact resulting in revival! Together, we can change the world.

ACTION

- Your prophetic destiny is real! It is time for the unlocking!
- Discover your intrinsic value.
- Find your place in the Body of Christ.
- Align yourself with a strong, prophetic Body of believers.
- Be trained and equipped for the ministry.

- Begin to edify, exhort and comfort others.

- Release the rivers of living water that reside in you.

- Do not be afraid to lift up your voice! Let your sound be heard!
- Build your daily worship altar to the Lord.

- Take your place each day at His gates!

- Arise and legislate according to His Word.

- Know that you are a carrier of the glory of God.

As you worship before the King, ask Him for a fresh outpouring of His glory that will unlock your prophet destiny! Then say, "Here am I Lord. Send me!"

References

All Scriptures NKJV
Word definitions from Strongs Concordance

Chapter 1
C. Peter Wagner
Lisa Beverly, Lioness Arising

Chapter 2
Glory of Zion International

Chapter 5
John Dickson, Chuck D. Pierce, Worship As It Is In Heaven
Dutch Sheets
Dr. Myles Munroe, ASAPH

Chapter 7
The Lock and Load Prophecies of God
James Mark Massa